Baptized into Wilderness

A Christian Perspective on
JOHN MUIR

RICHARD CARTWRIGHT AUSTIN

hn Knox Press
ATLANTA

ACKNOWLEDGMENTS

Scripture quotations from the Revised Standard Version of the Holy Bible, copyright, 1946, 1952, and © 1971, 1973 by the Division of Christian Education, National Council of the Churches of Christ in the U.S.A., are used by permission.

Excerpts from **The New English Bible** are copyright © the Delegates of the Oxford University Press and the Syndics of the Cambridge University Press, 1961, 1970. Reprinted by permission.

Excerpts from Edward W. L. Smith, *The Body in Psychotherapy* are reprinted by permission of McFarland & Co., Inc. Copyright 1985.

Excerpts from the John Muir Papers, Holt-Atherton Pacific Center for Western Studies, University of the Pacific. Copyright 1984 Muir-Hanna Trust.

Abbreviations:

JB	Jerusalem Bible
KJV	King James Version
NEB	New English Bible
RSV	Revised Standard Version

Library of Congress Cataloging-in-Publication Data

Austin, Richard Cartwright, 1934–
    Environmental theology.

    Bibliography: p.
    Includes index.
    Contents: v. 1. Baptized into wilderness.
    1. Nature—Religious aspects—Christianity. 2. Muir,
John, 1838–1914.   I.   Title.
BT695.5.A97   1987   231.7   87-45550
ISBN 0-8042-0869-7 (v. 1)

© copyright John Knox Press 1987
10 9 8 7 6 5 4 3 2 1
Printed in the United States of America
John Knox Press

Contents

Dedication

To the Devil's Fork watershed of Stony Creek,
in mountains above the Clinch River in southwestern Virginia.
It is returning to wildness.

Those who wished to build roads here,
to clearcut timber, to prospect for coal or uranium,
or to flood Devil's Fork behind a 300-foot high electric power dam,
have not been able to do so
because other people love this landscape
and respect the life of this place.

Introduction

May Christians find communion with nature? Or is nature part of "the world" from which the gospel calls us away? Does nature have a place in the worship of the Lord, or only in the worship of Baal and other pagan deities? Is our subjugation of other species and of the earth itself an expression of the image of God in humanity, or rather a violation of that image? Is rampant modern pollution of land, air, and water a tragic fulfillment of the human destiny charted in the Bible, or is it disobedience to the God who "loved the world so much" as to send Jesus (John 3:16, NEB)?

I have spent twenty-five years of Christian ministry in the ravaged coalfields of Appalachia where the earth bleeds from human oppression. People in my congregations opened my eyes to see that the land mattered in their spiritual health as well as in their physical welfare. For the past fifteen years the Presbyterian Church has excused me from the traditional responsibilities of pastoral ministry so I might explore how Christian faith relates to this environmental crisis. Working with other concerned citizens, I helped lead a nationwide effort to achieve federal legislation controlling strip mining for coal. I organized the people of Appalachia and the midwest who saved the Brumley Gap farming valley and Hidden Valley game lands from an electric utility that wished to flood them for the world's largest pumped-storage hydroelectric facility. On my small farm I grow strawberries, raise beef, and make maple syrup. Here I am nourished by mountain beauty while I try to understand how love and respect for nature may influence the way we live.

For several years I have been engaged in a comprehensive rethinking of Christian faith in the light of environmental responsibility. During this quest I discovered that in America we have had an advocate for nature whose spiritual insights rival those of Francis of Assisi for the Middle Ages: John Muir. Although Muir lived a century ago, he speaks to our time. His style is engaging, and more of his writing is available in print today than ever before.

John Muir (1838-1914) was the preeminent American in the early industrial era to identify himself with the shrinking wilderness and to speak relevantly in its defense to both the government and the popular imagination. Muir listened to the deepest voices in nature: not just to animals and plants, but to rocks and mountains. A skillful propagandist, he challenged America to find a place for the rights of the wild. "The world, we are told, was made especially for man—a presumption not supported by all the facts,"[1] wrote Muir, who became convinced that nature fully equaled civilization in value. He believed that modern men and women need wilderness for spiritual rebirth, and he also realized that nature needs social protection to survive the onslaught of industrial society.

Muir launched a twofold crusade. Promoting an out-of-doors gospel, he encouraged persons to reestablish contact with the wild. In addition he campaigned for government protection of natural resources in America. Cultivating his rustic personality, a "John Baptist" from the wilderness, Muir led the successful campaign to establish Yosemite National Park and was influential in generating public support for the National Park System. He founded the Sierra Club to defend the parks and to bring people into contact with wilderness. Many in high places sought him out; President Teddy Roosevelt, for example, went camping alone with him in Yosemite. Yet Muir's message contrasted with the dominant energies creating industrial America. He inspired an American environmental movement that continues to reflect his personality.

John Muir explored the heights of religious delight in nature. He has sometimes been characterized as a pantheist who rejected Christianity.[2] I will suggest, however, that Muir found Christ in Yosemite, in the glacier and the sequoia. They mediated to him the God who had been hidden by the severity of his strict Christian upbringing. Nature, by its intense presence, vitality, and beauty, demonstrated to Muir a value transcending the needs of human society. Muir responded to nature, and he answered God's call to be a voice for the wilderness. In that vocation he found life and meaning. He exhibited moral beauty.

After reading much of Muir's writing, as well as several fine modern studies of his thought and influence, I put my notebook in my pack and set out on the trails of Yosemite. It was late October, bright Indian summer, one of Muir's favorite seasons. I walked farther and climbed higher than I had anticipated. My mind cleared of chatter and my senses opened to the beauty around me, so that I could not contain my delight; on occasion I exploded with an involuntary whoop. Muir's explorations had been extraordinary. Mine were ordinary, and yet I knew the delight of transcending what I thought were my limits and seeing more than I guessed was there. Each morning I reviewed some of Muir's writings before setting out, and each day on the trail new insights came to consciousness. I wrote this book immediately after that communion with Muir's place and his spirit.

Knowledge alone will not protect nature, nor will ethics, for by themselves they do not arouse motivation strong enough to transform the exploitative patterns to which we have become accustomed. The protection of nature must be rooted in love and delight—in religious experience. I believe Christians may overcome historic hesitations about including nature in religious experience and may develop an appropriate religious understanding of nature.

Muir's own religious ecstasy, and the depth of his communion with nature challenge our capacity to follow. In 1870 Muir wrote the following letter with ink he made from cones of the giant sequoia, the more massive inland sister to the tall

coastal redwood. He shared one of his ecstatic moments of discovery with his closest confidante, Jeanne Carr.

Squirrelville
Sequoia Co
Nut Time

Dear Mrs. Carr   Do behold the King in his glory, King
Sequoia. Behold! Behold! seems all I can say. Some time ago I
left all for Sequoia: have been & am at his feet fasting & pray-
ing for light, for is he not the greatest light in the woods; in the
world. Where is such columns of sunshine, tangible, accessible,
terrestrialized. Well may I fast, not from bread but from busi-
ness, bookmaking, duty doing, & other trifles, & great is my
reward already for the manly treely sacrifice. What giant
truths since coming to gigantea, what magnificent clusters of
Sequoic *becauses*. From here I cannot recite you one, for you are
down a thousand fathoms deep in dark political quagg, but a
burr length less. But I'm in the woods woods woods, & they are
in *me-ee-ee*. The King tree & me have sworn eternal love—
sworn it without swearing & I've taken the sacrament with
Douglass Squirrell drank Sequoia wine, Sequoia blood, & with
its rosy purple drops I am writing this woody gospel letter. I
never before knew the virtue of Sequoia juice. Seen with sun-
beams in it, its color is the most royal of all royal purples. No
wonder the Indians instinctively drink it for they know not
what. I wish I was so drunk & Sequoical that I could preach the
green brown woods to all the juiceless world, descending from
this divine wilderness like a John Baptist eating Douglass
Squirrels & wild honey or wild anything, crying, Repent for the
Kingdom of Sequoia is at hand.

There is balm in these leafy Gileads; pungent burrs & living King-juice for all defrauded civilization; for sick grangers &
politicians.... Come Suck Sequoia & be saved.... I wish I were
wilder & so bless Sequoia I will be.... The sun is set & the star
candles are being lighted to show me & Douglass Squirrel to bed
therefore my Carr good night. You say, When are You Coming
down? Ask the Lord—Lord Sequoia.[3]

1. *Awakening*

The genius of John Muir combined keen perception, an inventive mind, and a remarkably agile physique. As the first son born to a family in Dunbar, Scotland, in 1838, Muir was wrapped in love from his mother, older sisters, and grandparents and thus gained a sense of security that he exercised even as a child with amazing feats of physical dexterity in the face of danger.[1] He also bore the full severity of Scottish patriarchy and Calvinism in the person of his father—a religious fanatic who became more unstable and brutal as young John grew. "In all the world," Muir would recall, "I know of nothing more pathetic and deplorable than a brokenhearted child, sobbing itself to sleep after being unjustly punished by a truly pious and conscientious misguided parent."[2]

Muir described his school days as a round of violence: learning by rote under the rod at school, receiving daily beatings at home for the slightest infraction, and constantly fighting among playmates who took out their frustrations on each other. Under the lash John was an excellent student. Fifty years later he observed, "I can't conceive of anything that would now enable me to concentrate my attention more fully than when I was a mere stripling boy, and it was all done by whipping." At home, "father made me learn so many Bible verses every day that by the time I was eleven years of age I had about three-fourths of the Old Testament and all of the New by heart and by sore flesh." He was also a fearless brawler among his companions.

> Nor could we be made to believe it was fair that father and teacher should thrash us so industriously for our good, while

> begrudging us the pleasure of thrashing each other for our good. ... If we did not endure our school punishments and fighting pains without flinching and making faces, we were mocked; ... therefore we at length managed to keep our features in smooth repose while enduring pain that would try anybody but an American Indian. ... One of our playground games was thrashing each other with whips about two feet long ... until one succumbed to the intolerable pain and thus lost the game.[3]

He escaped from this stern world by hunting birds' nests on the coastal cliffs or roaming the countryside around Dunbar.

In his eleventh year John's family emigrated to America, settling a virgin homestead in Wisconsin. The wilderness delighted John. His formal education was suspended as he and his younger brother were kept at work on the farm full time. In a few years his father would hand all the work to them and devote himself to Bible study and itinerant preaching. During late adolescence John developed the habit of rousing himself in the middle of the night to read until morning or to pursue his passion for inventing clocks and labor-saving machinery.

At age twenty-two Muir took some of his inventions to the state fair in Madison: a handmade wooden clock which could also light the morning fire automatically and awaken Muir by tilting the bed to stand him upright; and a thermometer based on an iron bar with dials so sensitive they responded to the body heat of an approaching person. His devices were a sensation, and Muir was regarded as a genius. The University of Wisconsin welcomed him and allowed him to follow his curiosity through the curriculum. He fell in love first with chemistry and then, more deeply, with botany.

When the government began draft calls to provide conscripts for the Civil War, John's younger brother fled to Canada. The Muirs were still Scottish citizens, and from their remote frontier perspective they did not identify with American political concerns. In the spring of 1864 John also left for Canada, anxious about the draft but also deferring a hasty decision to enter medical school. For six months he hid like a fugitive, alone in the woods and swamps north of Lake Huron. His consolation was collecting botanical samples.

One evening in June he was particularly lonely and anxious when at a stream bank he came upon a rare orchid (*Calypso borealis*), two white flowers against a background of yellow moss. Their beauty in such isolation gave him comfort: "They were alone. . . . I never before saw a plant so full of life; so perfectly spiritual, it seemed pure enough for the throne of its Creator. I felt as if I were in the presence of superior beings who loved me and beckoned me to come. I sat down beside them and wept for joy."[4] Separated from family, friends, and country, Muir felt the acceptance of the Creator mediated through these orchids. He would treasure this experience as one of the supreme moments of his life.

During the following three years Muir struggled to know his heart. His dream was to be a wandering botanist, but he needed money, and he also felt a moral obligation to follow a useful career. With his inventive genius Muir easily found work, first in a Canadian mill where he was offered a partnership, then at a wagon factory in Indianapolis where he also advanced rapidly. His inventiveness suited the needs of early industrial development. He received appreciation, and his work appeared useful. But at night Muir dreamed of botany. He wrote his sister,

> I am myself but a wandering star and move in as crooked an orbit as any star in the sky. I never before felt so *utterly homeless* as now. . . . I suppose that I am doomed to live in some of these noisy commercial centres. Circumstances over which I have had no control almost compel me to abandon the profession of my choice and to take up the business of an inventor, and now that I am among machines I begin to *feel* that I have some talent that way and so I almost think unless things change soon I shall turn my whole mind into that channel.[5]

In March 1867 Muir was repairing an industrial belt when his file slipped and punctured the cornea of his right eye. The shock blinded his left eye as well. When after a month of darkness his sight began to return, Muir knew what he would do. He vowed to take a "grand sabbath day three years long" to wander the world, so even if he must return to industry he might accumulate "a stock of wild beauty sufficient to lighten and brighten my after life in the shadows."[6] Six months later Muir, now twenty-nine, began his "sabbath" with a thousand-mile walk from Louisville, Kentucky, to Savannah, Georgia, and then across Florida to Cedar Key on the Gulf Coast. One biographer asserts that during this walk "Muir made a permanent break from Christianity."[7] This was, indeed, the time when he began to find his own footing spiritually as well as physically. He began to trust his own insights and worried less about reconciling them with the faith taught by his father.

Muir camped for a week in a "grand old forest graveyard" near Savannah where he waited, hungry and anxious, for a delayed money order from home. There he overcame a significant fear, concluding that death was not an enemy but a part of life.

> On no subject are our ideas more warped and pitiable than on death. Instead of the sympathy, the friendly union, of life and death so apparent in Nature, we are taught that death is an accident, a deplorable punishment for the oldest sin, the arch-enemy of life, etc. .... But let children walk with Nature, let them see the beautiful blendings and communions of death and life, their joyous inseparable unity, as taught in woods and meadows, plains and mountains and streams of our blessed star, and they will learn that death is stingless indeed, and as beautiful as life, and that the grave has no victory, for it never fights. All is divine harmony.[8]

In Florida, admiring a palm tree, Muir was able to reject the traditional distinction between human life and natural life. "They tell us," he noted, "that plants are not like man immortal, but are perishable—soul-less. I think that this is something that we know exactly nothing about."[9]   After a frightening encounter with an alligator, Muir reflected that such creatures have life and purpose independent of any usefulness to humanity: "Doubtless these creatures are happy, and fill the place assigned them by the great Creator of us all.

Fierce and cruel they appear to us, but beautiful in the eyes of God. . . . How narrow we selfish, conceited creatures are in our sympathies! how blind to the rights of all the rest of creation!"[10]

By the end of this walk Muir had come to the conviction that he need not accept the distorted priorities of civilization. He could be an advocate for other life. In his private journal he took a satisfying jab at Calvinist orthodoxy.

> Let a Christian hunter go the Lord's woods and kill his well-kept beasts, or wild Indians, and it is well; but let an enterprising specimen of these proper, predestined victims go to houses and fields and kill the most worthless person of the vertical god-like killers,—oh! that is horribly unorthodox, and on the part of the Indians atrocious murder! Well, I have precious little sympathy for the selfish propriety of civilized man, and if a war of races should occur between the wild beasts and Lord Man, I would be tempted to sympathize with the bears.[11]

At ease in the wilderness, Muir was anxious in the city. During a brief stopover in New York, awaiting passage to San Francisco, he stayed close to the dock. "I felt completely lost in the vast throngs of people." He saw the name "Central Park" on some streetcars but hesitated to visit the park "fearing that I might not be able to find my way back."[12] On his second day in San Francisco he "inquired of a man, who was carrying some carpenter's tools, the nearest way out of town to the wild part of the State."[13]

* * *

At age thirty, Muir visited the Yosemite valley for the first time. The next summer he obtained a shepherd's job in the surrounding mountains, and later he worked in the valley operating a sawmill and guiding tourists. Eventually his writings produced enough income to allow him full time for his explorations and studies. His five years in Yosemite formed him and shaped his mission.

In the mountains Muir experienced a distinctive physical mysticism through which he achieved remarkable contact with

his environment. During his first summer he wrote in his
journal,

> Now we are fairly into the mountains, and they are into us.
> We are fairly living now. What bright seething white-fire
> enthusiasm is bred in us—without our help or knowledge. A
> perfect influx into every pore and cell of us, fusing, vaporizing
> by its heat until the boundary walls of our heavy flesh taberna-
> cle seem taken down and we flow and diffuse into the very air
> and trees and streams and rocks, thrilling with them to the
> touch of the vital sunbeams. Responsive, we are part of nature
> now. . . . How glorious a conversion. . . .[14]

These experiences were grounded in intense sensuous perception. Muir found his bodily senses heightened. He wrote of "X-
rays of beauty that get into one thru bones and flesh."[15] Giving
his perceptions full attention and dedication, "literally gaping
with all the mouths of soul and body,"[16] he reached for his sur-
roundings in many strenuous, dangerous climbs. "One must
labor for beauty as for bread, here as elsewhere."[17]

Muir trusted his body, a trust he had developed through
a childhood of hard work and daring adventures. Furthermore
he trusted his contact with the earth.

> I like to walk, touch living Mother Earth—bare feet best, and
> thrill every step. Used to envy happy reptiles that had advan-
> tage of so much body in contact with earth, bosom to bosom.
> [We] live with our heels as well as head and most of our pleasure
> comes in that way.[18]

In his desire to experience nature more deeply, Muir will-
ingly set himself at great risk. He had now replaced fear of
death with a relish for life. Such a relish is an even better protector than fear, yet it inspires quite different patterns of behavior.
As a child Muir had known the heightened perception that
comes in moments of danger. Senses would lead where the mind
could not imagine. Of the many dangers Muir risked for the
reward of new perceptions, one of the clearest is his description
of nearly falling from the rock face of Mount Ritter.

> After gaining a point about half-way to the top, I was suddenly
> brought to a dead stop, with arms outspread, clinging close to
> the face of the rock, unable to move hand or foot either up or

down. My doom appeared fixed. I *must* fall. There would be a moment of bewilderment, and then a lifeless rumble down the one general precipice to the glacier below.

When this final danger flashed upon me, I became nerve-shaken for the first time since setting foot on the mountains, and my mind seemed to fill with a stifling smoke. But this terrible eclipse lasted only a moment, when life blazed forth again with preternatural clearness. I seemed suddenly to become possessed of a new sense. The other self, bygone experiences, Instinct, or Guardian Angel,—call it what you will,—came forward and assumed control. Then my trembling muscles became firm again, every rift and flaw in the rock was seen as through a microscope, and my limbs moved with a positiveness and precision with which I seemed to have nothing at all to do. Had I been borne aloft upon wings, my deliverance could not have been more complete.[19]

His perceptive skills quickly achieved a scientific harvest as well. During his first summer Muir noticed marks of glaciation on a canyon leading to Yosemite. "A fine discovery this," he noted in his journal.[20] After two years he had found enough such evidence to be convinced that all of Yosemite was the product of glaciers, challenging the accepted theory that the spectacular valley was the chasm formed by an earthquake. As his interpretation spread to scientific circles, Muir would achieve a reputation as the foremost expert on glaciers. He boasted of investigative technique which relied upon sensuous contact with nature rather than a predetermined scientific discipline.

This was my "method of study": I drifted about from rock to rock, from stream to stream, from grove to grove. Where night found me, there I camped. When I discovered a new plant, I sat down beside it for a minute or a day, to make its acquaintance and try to hear what it had to say. When I came to moraines, or ice-scratches upon the rocks, I traced them, learning what I could of the glacier that made them. I asked the boulders I met whence they came and whither they were going. I followed to their fountains the various soils upon which the forests and meadows are planted; and when I discovered a mountain or rock of marked form and structure, I climbed about it, comparing it with its neighbors, marking its relations to the forces that had acted upon it, glaciers, streams, avalanches, etc., in seeking to account for its form, finish, position, and general characters.[21]

In his fascination with the rock structure of Yosemite and the High Sierra, Muir developed a unique religious perspective which drew insight from the earthly and concrete. During his first summer he wrote of "these glorious old mountain days . . . so rocky and substantial yet so infinitely spiritual, exciting at once to work and rest, bestowing substance in its grandest forms."[22] He began to read the rocks with geological sensitivity; or rather, as he would say, they spoke to him as he learned to listen. When he returned to Yosemite from a trip, "all the rocks seemed talkative, and more lovable than ever. They are dear friends, and have warm blood gushing through their granite flesh; and I love them with a love intensified by long and close companionship."[23] The "warm blood" was the geologic life they exhibited—the creativity of God—which Muir could see with his "glacial eye."[24]

More than two centuries before, the Puritan theologian Jonathan Edwards had affirmed that "the beauties of nature are really emanations or shadows of the excellencies of the Son of God."[25] Now John Muir developed his perceptions of beauty into a similar notion of incarnation. "Rocks have a kind of life perhaps not so different from ours as we imagine. Anyhow their material beauty is only a veil covering spiritual beauty— a divine incarnation— instonation."[26]

During the summer and fall of 1871 Muir came to a sense of himself and his vocation. He ceased worrying about proving his usefulness to society—though it helped that he had been visited and praised by the geologist Joseph Le Conte and by his own literary idol, Ralph Waldo Emerson. Shedding the pressure from his family to enter a profession, he planned instead to follow where his communion with nature led him.

> There are eight members in our family. All are useful members of society—save me. . . . Surely, then, thought I, one may be spared for so fine an experiment. The remnants of compunction—the struggle concerning that serious business of settling down—gradually wasted and melted, and at length left me wholly free—born again!

> I will follow my instincts, be myself for good or ill, and see what will be the upshot. As long as I live, I'll hear waterfalls and birds and winds sing. I'll interpret the rocks, learn the language of flood, storm, and the avalanche. I'll acquaint myself with the glaciers and wild gardens, and get as near the heart of the world as I can.[27]

This new birth released a burst of energy so intense it worried friends who visited Muir. Like Jeremiah seized by a call from God, he was driven to know the glacial forces.

> Let me go only with God and his written rocks to guide me. . . . The grandeur of these forces and their glorious results overpower me, and inhabit my whole being. Waking or sleeping I have no rest. In dreams I read blurred sheets of glacial writing or follow lines of cleavage or struggle with the difficulties of some extraordinary rock form. Now it is clear that woe is me if I do not drown this tendency toward nervous prostration by constant labor in working up the details of this whole question. I have been down from the upper rocks only three days and am hungry for exercise already.[28]

By the end of 1871 John Muir, now thirty-three years old, had his own perspective on the world and a distinctive awareness of calling. Muir's sense of vocation included faith that God was protecting his steps so he might bring from the mountains truth his culture needed to hear. That November he wrote his mother,

> For the last two or three months I have worked incessantly among the most remote and undiscoverable of the deep cañons of this pierced basin, finding many a mountain page glorious with the writing of God and in characters that any earnest eye could read. . . . I know how Yosemite and all the other valleys of these magnificent mountains were made and the next year or two of my life will be occupied chiefly in writing their history in a human book—a glorious subject, which God help me preach aright. . . . In all my lonely journeys among the most distant and difficult pathless, passless mountains, I never wander, am never lost. Providence guides through every danger and takes me to all the truths which I need to learn, and some day I hope to show you my sheaves, my big bound pages of mountain gospel.[29]

2. *Christ in Nature*

In 1874 Muir received a letter from his father after he sent his parents an article about one of his risky adventures.

> MY VERY DEAR JOHN:
>
> Were you as really *happy* as my *wish* would make you, you would be permanently so in the *best* sense of the word. I received yours of the third inst. with your slip of paper, but I had read the same thing in "The Wisconsin," some days before I got yours, and then I *wished* I had not seen it, because it harried up my feelings so with another of your hair-breadth escapes. Had I seen it to be *God's work* you were doing I would have felt the *other* way, but I knew it was not God's work, although you seem to think you are doing God's service. If it had not been for God's boundless mercy you would have been cut off in the midst of your folly. All that you are attempting to show the *Holy Spirit* of God gives the believer to *see* at one glance of the eye, for according to the tract I send you they can see God's love, power, and glory in everything, and it has the effect of turning away their sight and eyes from the things that are seen and temporal to the things that are not seen and eternal, *according to God's holy word. . . .* You cannot warm the heart of the saint of God with your cold icy-topped mountains. O, my dear son, come away from them to the spirit of God and His holy word, and He will show our lovely Jesus unto you, who is by His finished work presented to you, without money and price. . . . And the best and soonest way of getting quit of the writing and publishing your book is to burn it, and then it will do no more harm either to you or others.[1]

Muir never made a public issue of how his spiritual insights related to Christianity, though after his dangerous climb of Mount Ritter, which had been a deeply religious experience, he wrote to a friend that "Christianity and Mountainanity are

streams from the same fountain."[2] Surely he knew that his
father's stinging rejection represented what he might expect
from many conservative Christians if he were to press the
issue. Despite his admiration for Thoreau and his friendship
with Emerson, Muir understood himself more in biblical terms
than in the language of Transcendentalism. (He could, as well,
attempt a humorous self-definition in the categories of learned
society: "self-styled poetico-trampo-geologist-bot. and ornith-
natural, etc.!!!"[3]) The image Muir favored and cultivated was
that of a *prophet* "descending from this divine wilderness like a
John Baptist," who could not only live in the wilderness but
speak *for* it, "crying, Repent for the Kingdom of Sequoia is at
hand."[4]

I recognize John Muir as a prophet speaking both to
American society and to the Christian community. Though
passionate in his religious conviction, Muir did not imagine
himself a theologian; he did not attempt to shape his religious
insights into a system to be integrated into Christianity or contrasted with it. Yet I hear the Lord speaking through Muir,
and this helps me respond to the natural world which Muir so
loved. This response, indeed, was the aim of Muir's prophetic
vocation.

To me the biblical notion of God implies a human vocation to express to nature, by our care of it, the justice and love of
God. Biblical ecology gives humanity a key role: to tend and
keep the earth with such faithfulness that all creation may be
inspired to praise the Lord. "The whole creation is eagerly waiting for . . . the children of God" (Romans 8:19, 21, JB). If we lose
contact with God, we lose touch with the source of our life and
the beauty of transcendent justice and compassion. If we lose
contact with nature, we lose touch with much of the joy of life
and an important part of our human calling. In either case the
human personality is incomplete, and human life is
impoverished.

Muir's special gift was listening to nature. He sat down
beside an unfamiliar plant "for a minute or a day, to make its
acquaintance and hear what it had to tell."[5] Attentive with his

full personality, Muir opened his most inward parts to his environment. Listening included analytical scrutiny from his botanical training, along with sensitivity to the plant's environmental relationships. Muir's listening to a plant also involved cultivating empathy—that intuitive projection by which we imagine the character of another. Together these techniques create the kind of understanding we hope for in human relationships: recognition of another's living integrity.

Beyond such recognition, Muir recommended an approach to nature even more radical, more religious:

> Independence is nowhere sweeter than in Yosemite. People who come here ought to abandon and forget all that is called business and duty, etc.; they should forget their individual existences, should forget they are born. They should as nearly as possible live the life of a particle of dust in the wind, or of a withered leaf in a whirlpool. They should come like thirsty sponges to imbibe without rule. It is blessed to lean fully and trustingly on Nature, to experience, by taking to her a pure heart and unartificial mind, the infinite tenderness and power of her love.[6]

When Muir urges losing oneself in the experience, I hear him suggesting that we lay aside the ego defenses that block experiences and also that we forego our common compulsion to process experience immediately into intellectual meaning. If we do not need to be looking for food, proof of a theory, God, or anything else, we may be able to take simple delight in our encounters with nature.

Yet to be as open to nature as Muir recommended—to risk one's security and identity—requires a particular religious perspective. In Muir's time some who were impressed with implications of Charles Darwin's theory of evolution through the survival of the fittest, saw nature primarily as a scene of combat. Muir, in contrast, saw in nature attributes which Christians see in Christ, "the infinite tenderness and power of her love."

Nature did function as Muir's "Christ"—the mediator who led him to God. His was not the normal route to the bibli-

cal Lord; for him the normal route was blocked. Muir had
memorized the Bible as a child and was immersed in the culture of Christianity, but his father's cruel piety twisted the
message. John Muir did not experience God's love through the
church and the other traditional instruments of Christian culture, because his father's interpretation of these instruments
distorted their meaning.

Fugitive, guilty, and alone, Muir found revived hope in
the solitary orchid which seemed "pure enough for the throne of
its Creator" and suggested "superior beings who loved me and
beckoned me to come." Through nature he began to trust God,
to calm his fear of death, and to develop insight, vitality, and
vocation. From Yosemite Muir wrote his brother, "I have not
been at church a single time since leaving home. Yet this glorious valley might well be called a church, for every lover of the
great Creator who comes within the broad overwhelming influ-
ences of the place fails not to worship as they never did before."[7]
If this is not everyone's experience, it was surely Muir's. In his
religious consciousness he fused experiences of nature with the
scriptural images stored in his memory from childhood.

*   *   *

I honor John Muir as a prophet. The prophetic vocation
may emerge when a person has achieved insight suggesting
resolution to a social tension which has become, for the prophet,
a personal tension as well. With such insight comes a burning
desire to share this new perspective. Muir knew delight in the
natural world, but he also felt the modern excitement in apply-
ing machinery to harness and control nature. The long "sabbath" which followed his accident was not just a retreat.
Learning from nature, Muir found motivation to engage again
with industrial society in an attempt to improve human understanding and to change public policies. Technology must be
guided by the claims of life. Industrial society, Muir proclaimed, must learn limits so all forms of life may continue
to thrive on the earth. When technology seeks to manipulate
everything, it has itself spun out of control.

Muir's religious insights were also rooted in a more inward struggle. Experiences of love and beauty, which his mother, his older sisters, and the natural world provided him, contrasted sharply with the violent, oppressive relationships which his father and his school characterized, patterns which society appeared to endorse. That same love and beauty were expressed in the religious images Muir absorbed in the Scriptures he memorized, yet these very images were forced upon him by a father who used them to justify cruelty and abuse. Muir encountered this pattern again in the factory, where Christian pieties were mouthed as justification for the exploitations of early capitalism. Repeatedly, biblical images and principles carried contradictory associations for the young man.

Resolving this inner tension was Muir's insight that nature is not a hierarchy but a communion. This was the message of "Lord Sequoia." Muir's vision was ecological: each served the needs of all, in death as well as in life. As Jesus had announced reversal of social hierarchies—"the last will be first, and the first last" (Matthew 20:16, RSV)—Muir reversed the common perception of natural hierarchies. He found life and spirit in rocks, as opposed to the material nature of "higher" beings, particularly people. Humanity was not superior to other species; before God such ranking was meaningless. In denying human superiority, Muir repudiated the human claim to exploit nature by right. Humanity must fit in, not dominate. "Lord Man" was a dangerous delusion.

Muir understood God from this same communal perspective. God was not a tyrant but a presence—as present to squirrels, flowers, and rocks as to men and women. Humans could not monopolize knowledge of God or seize God's authority. Muir had no doubt that God reigned, but that reign was without patriarchy, more immanent than transcendent. It was a creative, loving administration. By identifying God closely with nature, Muir also emphasized God's feminine characteristics. The masculine elements, caricatured by his father, Muir did not find in the cosmos; God could be trusted. I do not see Muir constructing a pantheism in the sense of finding within nature a new god to replace the biblical Lord. Rather, I see Muir finding insight through his experience of nature, to strip from his image of God the oppressive, patriarchal elements exemplified by his father. Jesus had rejected hierarchy and authority, preaching a social reversal which undermined patterns of human domination, but this image of Christ had since been captured and distorted by the church of Muir's father. Muir, in nature, found the earlier Christ again.

* * *

If American Christians can hear John Muir, we may recover a sense of our relation with nature which fits the gospel. We desperately need relationships with the natural world. We need communion with sequoia and Douglas Squirrel, and we need to express this communion within our religious forms so it may permeate our culture. Our isolation from nature inhibits the development of the image of God within us. Instead of bringing liberation to nature, we give vocal assent— or silent consent—to its oppression.

Yet Christ stands with the victim. I believe that "hungry or thirsty, a stranger or naked, sick or in prison" (Matthew 25:44, JB) now extends to what is eroded or polluted or endangered or valued only for human use. The world which we are abusing has become the body of our Lord. When we tear the earth needlessly, Christ suffers.

Modern Christians who addressed the great tree as "Lord Sequoia" would not be feeling the same holy awe felt by primitive people who stood helpless before its majesty and power. Our sense is more complex. The beauty of the sequoia may burn more deeply within us because we know how vulnerable it is to destruction unless we stand to save it. We may draw peace or strength from it, yet we must also give it peace, by lending our strength to its defense. Even the giant sequoia has become "one of the least of these" (Matthew 25:40, JB), vulnerable to greedy or thoughtless destruction. Here, in the crisis of the modern age, is a new potential for Christian communion, for reciprocal sharing, with nature.

We may say "Lord Sequoia" to acknowledge the presence of Christ who dwells with this tree, and who dwells also with the tiny and endangered snail darter and all others that are vulnerable. This is a moral presence. The sequoia is not the root of our faith, but the sequoia lays claim to our protection in Christ's name. Though its size and manifest beauty make it easier for us to respond, they are not the grounds for the claim. Quite simply, God made the tree and delights in it; and for this reason we are asked to bear towards the sequoia—and towards all nature—the image of God: protector, not destroyer.

3. *Spirituality*

One bright October night in 1871, John Muir camped in the Yosemite high country by Lake Nevada and watched the reflections of trees and mountains in the still water. He jotted notes about how the reflections showed "every line, every shadow in fine neutral tint, clear, intensely pure" in the "rayless, beamless light." Moonlit Yosemite domes shone on the surface of the lake.

> The glacier-polish of rounded brows [is] brighter than any mirror, like windows of a house shining with light from the throne of God—to the very top a pure vision in terrestrial beauty.... It is as if the lake, mountain, trees had souls, formed one soul, which had died and gone before the throne of God, the great First Soul, and by direct creative act of God had all earthly purity deepened, refined, brightness brightened, spirituality spiritualized, countenance, gestures made wholly Godful! ... I spring to my feet crying: "Heavens and earth! Rock is not light, not heavy, not transparent, not opaque, but every pore gushes, glows like a thought with immortal life."[1]

Muir had begun to read rocks, tracing the creativity of the glaciers which had polished the domes and cut the valleys, preparing the earth for the life and beauty now apparent. This exciting night Muir grasped that the most essential characteristic of rock was not something which could be weighed or measured, but was this very capacity to transmit and support life. Rocks joined in God's creativity.

The biblical Lord is distinctively worldly, intervening in the world's activities aggressively and insisting upon justice and compassion. God's delight in each creative act and God's regard for the welfare of all creatures are also manifest in the

Bible. In the Christian tradition, however, the place of nature in this worldly perspective has not been expressed adequately.

In Muir's time the expansive ethos of the industrial revolution permeated society. Humanity felt powerful. The followers of Charles Darwin portrayed the struggle for existence as an evolution upward toward the human—the species most fit to inhabit the earth. Darwinians and Christians might argue over the creative process, but they both placed humanity at the same height, "little less than a god," crowned with glory and honor (Psalm 8:5, NEB). Both implicitly endorsed human striving to protect and extend human dominance.

Although agreeing with Darwin's theory of evolution, Muir drew quite different spiritual inferences when he looked at evolution from his geological perspective.

What is "higher," what is "lower" in Nature? We speak of higher forms, higher types, etc., in the fields of scientific inquiry. Now all of the individual "things" or "beings" into which the world is wrought are sparks of the Divine Soul variously clothed upon with flesh, leaves, or that harder tissue called rock, water, etc.

Now we observe that, in cold mountain altitudes, Spirit is but thinly and plainly clothed. As we descend down their many sides to the valleys, the clothing of all plants and beasts and of the forms of rock becomes more abundant and complicated. When a portion of Spirit clothes itself with a sheet of lichen tissue, colored simply red or yellow, or gray or black, we say that is a low form of life. Yet is it more or less radically Divine than another portion of Spirit that has gathered garments of leaf and fairy flower and adorned them with all the colors of Light, though we say that the latter creature is of a higher form of life? All of these varied forms, high and low, are simply portions of God radiated from Him as a sun, and made terrestrial by the clothes they wear, and by the modifications of a corresponding kind in the God essence itself. The more extensively terrestrial a being becomes, the higher it ranks among its fellows, and the most terrestrial being is the one that contains all the others, that has, indeed, flowed through all the others and borne away parts of them, building them into itself. Such a being is man, who has flowed down through other forms of being and absorbed and assimilated portions of them into himself, thus becoming a

> microcosm most richly Divine because most richly terrestrial, just as a river becomes rich by flowing on and on through varied climes and rocks, through many mountains and vales, constantly appropriating portions to itself, rising higher in the scale of rivers as it grows rich in the absorption of the soils and smaller streams. . . .[2]

This paragraph expresses a striking paradox: the path to God leads in two directions, "up" to mountain heights where "Spirit is but thinly and plainly clothed," and "down" to humanity which evolved as a "microcosm most richly Divine because most richly terrestrial."

In the Bible one can see a similar paradox. God is expressed in images of simple energy, such as "spirit" and "light." Yet God is also revealed as a complex Personality, known most fully not when detached from the earth but when incarnate in Jesus. At their best, biblical religions can magnificently evoke God's personality so the Lord remains relevant to persons and cultures in each age. Western Christianity, however, is often less imaginative in conveying the simplicity of God—the Spirit—who may shrink to a vagueness which can be experienced only by the mystic.

Muir suggested that the path to the Spirit is not *away* from the world but deeper *into* the world, deeper into communion with nature and with the primary forces where Spirit is lightly clothed. Probing the simplest elements to discover their full character and vitality, he developed an incarnational understanding of the Spirit which complements the traditional Christian understanding of God's personality incarnate in Jesus. Thus Muir brought to life again both the religious image of God's spirit and the sensuous experience of God's beauty.

Within Muir's spiritual ecology, humanity is not at a lower level but at a place different from that imagined by the enthusiasts of technological progress. In the evolution "down" to men and women, traces of all things are deposited in the human flesh and personality. People, therefore, have the greatest potential for communion with all forms of life and with the earth. If that communion is realized, humans are the most divine, drawing closest to God's own perspective and delight.

> Man is so related to all of Nature, that he is builded of small worlds. When God made man "of the dust of the earth" he put into the compound fields and forests complete. All the mountain ranges of the world. Suns and moons and all animals and plants and minerals. ... [H]e is a bundle of worlds which lie calm until stirred by the appearance of the material symbol. Thus "all of Nature is found in man."[3]

God loves the earth, gives to it, and gives to us through it. By acknowledging our earthly character we claim our distinctive place as children of God, called to tend and care for the world which delights our Lord.

Muir's philosophies of nature and spirituality were themselves ecological constructions. Different aspects of nature led Muir to different insights. As a writer he wisely kept his insights clothed in the life they sprang from, leading his readers to commune with the glacier, the rock, the waterfall, the sequoia, and the wild sheep. Related insights formed an understanding. Muir began his spiritual pilgrimage observing individual flowers, rocks, and trees. He then came to see the landscape as a living history and incarnation of God's spirit. After the ancient glaciers had advanced and then receded, "the young rocks glowed like silver, waterfalls began their anthems, waving pines flocked to their appointed places in the groves, the warm air blossomed with insects, and the mission of the ice was accomplished."[4]

Muir's spiritual pilgrimage, however, did not stop at the oneness experienced by Eastern mystics. He continued to a truly biblical vision of the Lord who delights in creating other lives— lives with distinctiveness, individuality, and vitality of their own. The beauty of God's creativity is manifest when each flower, rock, tree, and person shines with its own vitality, yet depends upon all and contributes to all in an ecology of life. Muir's spiritual imagination completed this journey of insight. When simple sense-perception builds toward analysis and intuition,

> the tendency is to unification. We at once find ourselves among eternities, infinitudes, and scarce know whether to be happy in the sublime simiplicity of radical causes and origins or whether to be sorry on losing the beautiful fragments which we thought perfect and primary absolute units; but as we study and mingle with nature more, the pain caused by the melting of all beauties into one First Beauty disappears, because, after their first baptismal submergence in fountain God, they go again washed and clean into their individualisms, more clearly defined than ever, unified yet separate.[5]

Muir drew spiritual nourishment from earthquake, wind, and flood. In the Old Testament such forces were seen to herald God's presence, but most modern Christians have lost this awareness. From our human-centered perspective we see these natural forces only as tragedies.

When God approached Moses on Sinai, "the whole mountain quaked greatly" (Exodus 19:18, RSV). Isaiah warned Jerusalem that "punishment shall come from the LORD of Hosts with thunder and earthquake" (Isaiah 29:6, NEB). Earthquake displayed God's elemental vitality; it redistributed things, sometimes for the better. The prophet Haggai heard God say on the site of the ruined Jerusalem temple, "Once again, in a little while, I will shake the heavens and the earth and the sea and the dry land; and I will shake all nations, so that the treasures of all nations shall come in, and I will fill this house with splendor" (Haggai 2:6-7, RSV).

When Muir was in Yosemite in March 1872, the valley was struck by the great Inyo earthquake: "I ran out of my cabin, near the Sentinel Rock, both glad and frightened, shouting, 'A noble earthquake!' feeling sure I was going to learn something."[6] As rocks tumbled from the towering cliffs most people fled the valley, but Muir remained to enjoy "the most sublime storm I ever experienced." He reported, "It is delightful to be trotted and dumpled on our Mother's mountain knee."[7] It was "as if God had touched the mountains with a muscled hand or were wearing them upon him as common bones & flesh."[8] Muir set out pails of water to help him analyze shock patterns during the aftershocks, and afterward he prepared

both popular and scientific essays on the experience. Years
later he interpreted the earthquake as nature's way of redis-
tributing beauty.

> Some of the streams were completely dammed; driftwood,
> leaves, etc., gradually filling the interstices between the boul-
> ders, thus giving rise to lakes and level reaches; and these
> again, after being gradually filled in, were changed to mead-
> ows, through which the streams are now silently meandering;
> while at the same time some of the taluses took the places of old
> meadows and groves. Thus rough places were made smooth,
> and smooth places rough. ... All Nature's wildness tells the
> same story—the shocks and outbursts of earthquakes ... are
> the orderly beauty-making love-beats of Nature's heart.[9]

Muir was impatient that so few could enjoy nature at its
most energetic. To him, a flood was a benevolent act, renewing
the earth.   After enjoying a fine flood in 1875, he observed
sadly that "it will doubtlessly be remembered far more for the
drifted bridges and houses that chanced to lie in its way than
for its own beauty, or for the thousand thousand blessings it
brought to the fields and gardens of nature."[10] Muir asked his
readers to stretch their empathy beyond human loss to measure
the gain brought by flood to the whole community of life. More
than that, Muir enticed his readers to see a flood from the point
of view of the water itself—rushing, exulting, liberated from
confinement.

> ... morning saw Yosemite in the glory of flood. Torrents of
> warm rain were washing the valley walls, and melting the
> upper snows of the surrounding mountains; and the liberated
> waters held jubilee.[11]

Muir was like the psalmist who urged nature to delight
in self-expression

> Let the floods clap their hands: let the hills be joyful together
>   Before the LORD. (Psalm 98:8, 9, KJV)

Where others project agony onto nature—imagining, for example, that trees suffer when whipped by a gale—Muir projected
joy. In a windstorm, he noted, "the force of the gale was such

that the most steadfast monarch [of the giant Silver Pines] rocked down to its roots with a motion plainly perceptible when one leaned against it. Nature was holding high festival, and every fiber of the most rigid giants thrilled with glad excitement." Muir's own enjoyment matched that of nature.

> I drifted on through the midst of this passionate music and motion, across many a glen, from ridge to ridge; often halting in the lee of a rock for shelter, or to gaze and listen. Even when the grand anthem had swelled to its highest pitch, I could distinctly hear the varying tones of individual trees;—Spruce, and Fir, and Pine, and leafless Oak,—and even the infinitely gentle rustle of the withered grasses at my feet. Each was expressing itself in its own way,—singing its own song, and making its own peculiar gestures,—manifesting a richness of variety to be found in no other forest I have yet seen.[12]

During this particular storm, Muir entered communion more deeply than he had before. He climbed one hundred feet to the top of a young Douglas fir to ride out the gale.

> The slender tops fairly flapped and swished in the passionate torrent, bending and swirling backward and forward, round and round, tracing indescribable combinations of vertical and horizontal curves, while I clung with muscles firm braced, like a bobolink on a reed.
>
> In its widest sweeps my tree-top described an arc of from twenty to thirty degrees, but I felt sure of its elastic temper, having seen others of the same species still more severely tried—bent almost to the ground indeed, in heavy snows—without breaking a fiber. I was therefore safe, and free to take the wind into my pulses and enjoy the excited forest from my superb outlook.[13]

By this time, 1878, Muir was sensitive to the challenge of communicating with the public, preparing essays on his experiences which came to be known as "Stormy Sermons." He assumed a prophetic stance in the image of his hero, "John Baptist." And, like prophets in the Old Testament, he fashioned not only words but also symbolic acts to convey the truth of his perspective to those who might never climb a tree. In full communion with the storm, he spoke with authority.

The varied gestures of the multitude were seen to fine advantage, so that one could recognize the different species at a distance of several miles by this means alone, as well as by their forms and colors, and the way they reflected the light. All seemed strong and comfortable, as if really enjoying the storm, while responding to its most enthusiastic greetings. We hear much nowadays concerning the universal struggle for existence, but no struggle in the common meaning of the word was manifest here; no recognition of danger by any tree; no deprecation; but rather an invincible gladness as remote from exultation as from fear.[14]

Muir projected onto the forest the emotions he felt. He did so through clinging to the trees, feeling their movements, listening to their sounds, and entering as deeply as he could into relationship with them. Is this not how we learn to know a beloved friend? This approach honors the life of the earth as "scientific" detachment never can, revealing what the detached observer will never discover. For those who still doubted the joy of trees in the storm, Muir had a final, telling argument: the healthy, diverse, beautiful forest that such storms help to produce. When we see that "the manifest result of all this wild storm-culture is the glorious perfection we behold; then faith in Nature's forestry is established, and we cease to deplore the violence of her most destructive gales, or of any other storm-implement whatsoever."[15]

In the Bible the wind and the Holy Spirit are closely associated. Since both Hebrew and Greek use the same word to mean spirit and wind, it is sometimes difficult to know which meaning is intended. Jesus seemed to use this word in both ways when, after telling Nicodemus "You must be born over again," he continued,

The *wind* blows where it wills; you hear the sound of it, but you do not know where it comes from, or where it is going. So with everyone who is born from *spirit* (John 3:7, 8, NEB, italics added).

If we fear wind, do we also fear the Spirit, and new birth? They are not the same, but fearfulness may block our access to each.

Nature, Muir believed, offers an antidote to our fears. The antidote is not to test one's faith by enduring a storm; Muir's treetop climb was a prophetic witness, not an example for the beginner. Rather, the antidote is to begin opening one's senses to the world and to begin trusting awareness and expression—nature's expression and one's own.

The Spirit begins as a gentle breeze.

4. *Sensuousness*

John Muir exhibited a distinctive combination of physical expressiveness and spiritual discernment. Western thought tends to dissociate these characteristics, separating the soul from the body, the spiritual from the material. When Christianity spread from Palestine through the Roman world, it adopted this dualistic perspective. However, I want to affirm the fundamental unity of physical and spiritual experience. I believe that vitality, imagination, creativity, and transcendence all spring from personality when one is physically expressive, self-accepting, and engaged with culture and environment. The life of such a person, met by God, may express moral beauty.

In his striking physical dexterity and sensory acuteness, John Muir related sensuously with the earth and many forms of life. He achieved scientific, ethical, and spiritual insights, and conveyed them with affecting words and engaging actions, influencing his era. A healthy, whole person, Muir had the vitality and commitment of one "born over again" (John 3:3, NEB).

Jesus himself displayed such wholeness. Frequently he admonished, "He who has ears to hear, let him hear," implying that the *sensibility* of his hearers—the openness of senses and feelings—conditioned their capacity to receive his message. He used vivid images and emotive parables to reach people.

One of Jesus' beatitudes joins together his psychology and spirituality: "How blest are those whose hearts are pure; they shall see God" (Matthew 5:8, NEB). Jesus did not mean those who are sinless; he came to bring sinners to God, not the perfect. Rather, he meant those who really desire, those who are single-minded, those who are not faking. Having purity of heart implies that we know our true feelings and express them, neither masking ourselves for others nor hiding our feelings below our own awareness. From this type of expressiveness derive engaging love and vital life. Jesus taught that to achieve such directness we may need to be "born over again" (John 3:3, NEB), reopening our personality from the core and rebuilding from the beginning. One reason Jesus is so treasured is that he evidently lived the transparent purity of heart about which he preached. He expressed the capability of the human personality.

Writing about a walk through a glacier meadow, John Muir summoned readers to discover their full personality. He engages our sensuous imagination. He entices us away from the repressions endemic to city life and civil society, where we believe we must control our feelings.

> ... these wild lawns, with all their exquisite fineness, have no trace of that painful, licked, snipped, repressed appearance that pleasure-ground lawns are apt to have. . . . [T]hey respond to the touches of every breeze, rejoicing in pure wildness, blooming and fruiting in the vital light.

Continuing, Muir asks us not to fear but to relax in the gentle security of nature's beauty.

> With inexpressible delight you wade out into the grassy sun-lake, feeling yourself contained in one of Nature's most sacred chambers, withdrawn from the sterner influences of the mountains, secure from all intrusion, secure from yourself, free in the universal beauty. . . . Bees hum as in a harvest noon, butterflies waver above the flowers, and like them you lave in the vital sunshine, too richly and homogeneously joy-filled to be capable of partial thought. You are all eye, sifted through and through with light and beauty. Sauntering along the brook that meanders silently through the meadow from the east, special flowers call you back to discriminating consciousness.[1]

Muir understood that sensuous engagement was a key to spiritual renewal. In his day, some religious movements supported this perspective. The religion of the polite, inspired by Ralph Waldo Emerson and the Transcendentalists, endorsed a refined aesthetic and a sensuous expressiveness, and the dominant revivalism of the masses was frankly and enthusiastically emotional. Yet then as now, many people had been taught to fear their feelings. Some were schooled in scientific detachment, some disciplined by the needs of industry, and some trained to hide sexual desires. Religion for them was associated more with the limiting of experience and the control of feelings than with expression.

Wishing to push engagement with nature beyond the limits with which romantics and Transcendentalists were comfortable, Muir rejected John Ruskin's notion of "aesthetic distance," which held that the appreciation of natural beauty depended upon civilized separation.[2] He was disappointed when he could not persuade his beloved but aging Emerson to abandon a hotel bed and camp with him under the giant sequoia.[3] Furthermore, Muir pointedly rejected the idea that detached, unemotional observation was necessary for scientific understanding. After leading his readers through the glacier meadow, he commented,

> The influences of pure nature seem to be so little known as yet, that it is generally supposed that complete pleasure of this kind, permeating one's very flesh and bones, unfits the student for scientific pursuits in which cool judgment and observation are required. But the effect is just the opposite. Instead of producing a dissipated condition, the mind is fertilized and stimulated and developed like sun-fed plants.[4]

To reach his pioneering geological conclusions Muir used both sensitive observation and sensuous historical imagination, recapturing the motions, sights, and sounds of prior ages.

> Nothing goes unrecorded ... though human eye cannot detect the handwriting of any but the heaviest. Every event is both written and spoken. The wing marks the sky as well as making stir in sounding words, and the winds all feel it and know it and tell it. Glaciers make the deepest mark of any eroding agent, and write their histories in inerasable lines. And as

we can in some measure read and recall the forms and songs of dried-up streams by walking in their channels, so we can read the history of glaciers by tracing their channels centuries after they have vanished. And here the difficulty is not so much on account of dimness as of magnitude; the characters are so large it is difficult to see them from top to bottom in one view.[5]

Muir became aware that human senses register only a small band of the sounds and sights which exist in nature, and that our consciousness can process only a limited number of these into understandable images. Imagination may help us break through these limits to establish sensuous contact with more of natural life.

We hear only woodpeckers and squirrels and the rush of turbulent streams. But imagination gives us the sweet music of tiniest insect wings, enables us to hear . . . the vibration of every needle, the waving of every bole and branch, the sound of stars in circulation like particles in the blood. . . . Imagination is usually regarded as a synonym for the unreal. Yet is true imagination healthful and real, no more likely to mislead than the coarser senses.[6]

Such sounds may not be measurable by acoustic devices, but the image conveys truth. Imaginative engagement with the world's life is more true than the assumption of silence.

*   *   *

Both oppression and repression can damage human capacities to receive sensation and to feel emotion. Life can be painful and people can be cruel; in self-defense we may harden ourselves, like young Muir in school, so we feel less pain. Thus hardened, we also have more difficulty feeling pleasure. And if our parents or others have alarmed us about our deepest desires, we may hold them in check so we neither feel them nor show them. Such repression dulls our capacity to engage with life.

Jesus rejected the approach to morality which would cover seething inner impulses with a shell of conformity—what we would call repression: "You clean the outside of cup and dish, which you have filled inside by robbery and self-indulgence! ... You are like tombs covered with whitewash; they look well from outside, but inside they are full of dead men's bones and all kinds of filth" (Matthew 23:25, 27, NEB). He asked us to resist the quick moral fix, to search instead for the birth of insight to unite our deepest desires with the beauty of moral purpose. He urged us to take the risks of feeling, to engage with life and with God. "How blest are the sorrowful. ... How blest are those who hunger and thirst. ... How blest are those who know their need of God; the kingdom of Heaven is theirs" (Matthew 5:4, 6, 3, NEB). Loving, with the risk of disappointment, is better than not caring. Jesus' example suggests that it may be better to risk pain, even death, than to live without feeling.

Muir remembered his childhood burden of oppression, and with particular bitterness he remembered how misguided religion could imprison the spirit. A friend sent him a catalogue from the severe church school where she taught, and it led him to imagine "a den of ecclesiastical slave-drivers," whose "grizzly thorny ranks of cold enslaving 'musts' made me shudder as I fancy I should had I looked into a dungeon."[7] In a firm and loving letter Muir encouraged his friend to break free from self-punishment and depression, and to escape.

> I hope you will not persist in self-sacrifice of so destructive a species. ... I know very well how you toil and toil, striving against lassitude and the cloudy weather of discouraging cares with a brave heart, your efforts toned by the blessedness of doing good; but do not, I pray you, destroy your health. The Lord understands his business and has plenty of tools, and does not require overexertion of any kind.

> I wish you could come here and rest a year in the simple unmingled love fountains of God. ... He flows in grand undivided currents, shoreless and boundless over creeds and forms and all kinds of civilizations and peoples and beasts, saturating all.[8]

* * *

Wholly unlike his memories of oppressive religion, Muir's description of mountain climbing reads almost like an account of sexual intercourse. This is not surprising, since either experience may release vitality from the deepest core of human personality in a fully satisfying engagement with another.

I find that human expression moves from desire to engagement to satisfaction. Wilhelm Reich analyzed this progression in the 1930s in his studies of sexual orgasm. There he observed a sequence of TENSION→ CHARGE→DISCHARGE→ RELAXATION which he believed is fundamental to the expressiveness of all organisms and indeed to many inorganic processes as well.[9] Edward W. L. Smith, in more recent characterization of this same pattern, places more emphasis on the contact with another. He suggests that the "contact episode" has three stages of growing awareness, followed by three of expression: WANT → AROUSAL→ EMOTION → ACTION→ INTERACTION → SATISFACTION. The progression starts with a desire which arouses energy and feeling; then a person acts to find another with whom to interact so the desire may be satisfied.[10] Disappointment or failure can occur in any of these stages. The food which can fulfil my hunger may not be available; my interaction with another may be frustrated. I may so fear certain desires as not to feel them; I may hide them under substitute desires. I may feel vague urges and not know what I want, or I may lack the energy to rise to action. I may be so anxious that even a completed experience fails to satisfy.

The person who is able to complete an engaging experience feels satisfied and strengthened for continued living. When contact is frustrated and incomplete, however, the withdrawn person carries the burden of this discouragement which makes renewed contact more difficult. Jesus recognized that when people are unable to hear, feel, or act with integrity, life withers. It needs rebirth.

Few of us express ourselves fully in every relationship. When we do make contact and achieve satisfaction, however, our lives expand. For John Muir, satisfaction came from taking walks, seeing and feeling nature, and, particularly, climbing mountains.

Muir's love affair with mountains was so intense it seemed physiological. "I think that one of the *properties* of that compound which we call man," he wrote in 1872, "is that when exposed to the rays of mountain beauty it glows with *joy*."[11] Muir described climbing as "every muscle in harmonious accord, thrilled and toned and yielding us the very highest pleasures of the flesh."[12] When his senses were sharpened by danger, or by joy, he moved without deliberation—a psychophysical unity.   His recommended technique for descending a talus slope of rock and debris was to run downward—the rhythm of the feet discovering, without reflection, pattern in the random placement of boulders. He covered prodigious distances in a day; the hikes he recommends in his book on Yosemite are nearly impossible for even the most physically fit in the time he suggests.[13] He seems to have moved almost like the mountain sheep he loved. A friend observed him climb.

> Muir began to *slide* up that mountain. I had been with mountain climbers before, but never one like him. A deer lope over the smoother slopes, a sure instinct for the easiest way into a rocky fortress, an instant and unerring attack, a serpent-like glide up the steep; eye, hand and foot all connected dynamically; with no appearance of weight to his body.[14]

Most importantly, through climbing Muir reached satisfaction. He could truly rest in the alpine meadow when he descended.

> It is in these garden dells and glades, in peaceful spots where the winds are quiet, holding their breath, and every lily is motionless on its stem, that one is wholly free to enjoy self-forgetting. Here is no care, no time, and one seems to float in the deep, balmy summertide after being thoroughly awakened and exhilarated by the dangers and enjoyments by some grand excursion into the thin deeps of the sky among the peaks.[15]

Although he was the first to scale several High Sierra peaks, Muir ridiculed the notion of "conquering" a mountain. His communion was discovery, love, and respect. "When a mountain is climbed it is said to be conquered—as well say a man is conquered when a fly lights on his head."[16] But he stressed an element of the completed experience which—as part of a happy withdrawal—could be added as a seventh element to the psychological cycle sketched above: → MEMORY, which builds the experience into the growing fiber of one's being.

> These beautiful days must enrich all my life. They do not exist as mere pictures—maps hung upon the walls of memory to brighten at times when touched by association or will, only to sink again like a landscape in the dark; but they saturate themselves into every part of the body and live always.[17]

5. *Moral Beauty*

I have used the phrase *moral beauty* without explanation. My conception of moral beauty combines aesthetic, ecological, and religious dimensions of the experience of beauty. To experience beauty is to experience another positively, both in emotional awareness and in ecological relationship. I do not see beauty if I feel alienated. When I do see beauty, there is a relationship, a context. Therefore, the "beautiful other"—a person, a tree, a painting—matters to me. I value the other and I am drawn toward it in this meaningful context. There are many ways in which my needs and my fears may cause distortion, but the experience of beauty encourages a relationship of affection, respect, and responsibility. *Moral beauty* expresses the quality of this relationship.[1]

John Muir understood that the experience of beauty was the fruit of positive involvement. The beauty of a scene grows as one's relationship with it deepens. Muir's meditation on this point followed a trip where he took two artists into the mountains to paint and then left them for his famous, risky climb up Mount Ritter.

> When looking for the first time from an all-embracing standpoint like this, the inexperienced observer is oppressed by the incomprehensible grandeur of the peaks, and it is only after they have been studied one by one, long and lovingly, that their far-reaching harmonies become manifest. Then, penetrate the wilderness where you may, the main telling features to which all the topography is subordinate are quickly perceived, and the most ungovernable Alp-clusters stand revealed, regularly fashioned, and grouped like works of art,—eloquent monuments of the ancient ice-rivers that brought them into relief.[2]

The experience of beauty is not simply the result of the human subject moving to engage with something, or someone, beautiful. The beautiful actually calls to us; it reaches toward us to engage us. Beauty is self-giving.

"One thing have I asked of the LORD ... to behold the beauty of the LORD" (Psalm 27:4, RSV). This is David's prayer in the Psalms. Beauty expresses the distinctiveness of the God revealed in the Bible: creative, self-giving, engaged. The Lord creates multitudes of others and delights in them. Creatures receive vitality, individuality, even autonomy. However, the Lord sets us in a world where we need each other and asks us to relate to each other to support life. The Lord calls for justice and compassion, within species and among species.

The beauty of the Lord undergirds the existence of God. That is, the Lord becomes real to me when I experience the beauty in God's gift of life and when I find my own place and purpose within the ecology of life. Then I experience something of the moral beauty of God and hear the claims of justice and compassion. I believe.

Writing in his notebook sometime during his journey with the two artists, John Muir expressed God's beauty this way:

> All of Gods universe is glass to the soul of light. Infinitude mirrors reflecting all receiving all. The Stars whirl and eddy and boil in the currents of the ocean called space. . . . Trees in camplight and grasses and weeds impressive beyond thought so palpably Godful in form and in wind motion. . . . The pines spiring around me higher higher to the Star-flowered sky are plainly full of God. . . . Oh the infinite abundance and universality of Beauty. Beauty is God. What shall we say of God that we may not say of Beauty.[3]

Biblically it is appropriate to join God and beauty so intimately. The distinctiveness of the biblical Lord is that God is not detached or self-absorbed, but engaged and self-giving. This is the beauty of the Lord. However, I would suggest one change in Muir's expression. It is not adequate to say "Beauty is God." It is precise to say "God is beauty." This parallels the biblical declarations that "God is spirit" (John 4:24, RSV) and "God is love" (I John 4:8, KJV), along with Jesus' assertion, "I am the way, the truth, and the life" (John 14:6, KJV). God is not just a quality in relationships. God, in the biblical understanding, is a distinct, vital, complex Personality. Beauty is a perspective on God's heart, characterizing the Personality who sustains the world we know. The life and relationships that God creates, invites us to experience, and calls us to sustain and protect are the beauty of the world.

* * *

The genius of John Muir's politics, as we shall see, was that he did not try to save the wilderness by keeping humanity away from it. Rather, he tried to help humans become a part of wilderness, in order to save both. Only when humans and nature become parts of an integrated ecology will all be whole.

In Muir's ecological perception, everything was beautiful. "None of Nature's landscapes are ugly so long as they are wild."[4] Everything had a place, relationships, and purpose. The wilderness was perfect. It was not unchanging, but all things had a place and contributed to its beauty. The giant sequoia was a climax species in portions of the High Sierra forest. This ancient tree was not just the culmination of the present ecology, but a participant in several, quite different ecologies through the ages. Each was a perfection in the sense that each was whole. In each the sequoia had a place, towering, using the environment, yet also used and useful. It was beautiful.

Muir helps me understand the place of humanity in relation to nature, and particularly in relation to wilderness. Muir saw the beauty of Yosemite and took delight in it. He did this directly, with his full sensory capacities, as an engaged human observer, and he also experienced it indirectly, through complex ecological intuitions. Imaginatively entering the experience of the Douglas squirrel among the trees, the water ouzel in the rushing rapids, and the mountain sheep among the peaks, Muir sought to see the environment through their eyes and to share their delight. He rejoiced with the waters in their flood-time liberation, waved with the trees in the storm. He listened to the rocks talking and recreated the experience of the glacier.

We know some species have sensory capacities which humans lack. Indeed, there may be many more sensibilities in nature than we imagine. Similarly, with his reflective capacities, Muir could experience the relationships of the Douglas squirrel in ways the squirrel itself could not. Muir could see ecologically and historically, and he could be analytical; but he never allowed analysis to distance him from those with whom he communed.

Muir's presence with all his human faculties, his recognition of beauty, his delight and praise, enriched the ecology. Although never intrusive, Muir entered fully into the place and became part of the High Sierra's reflection upon itself, helping Yosemite rejoice in its own beauty.   Refusing to hide in Yosemite, Muir instead helped human society fashion ways to experience the wilderness without destroying it. He expressed moral beauty.

The distinctive quality of John Muir's presence enriched the Yosemite landscape. He showed how humans might relate to wilderness with integrity, benefiting both nature and the human participants. As he heard the rocks and rejoiced with the waters, he brought past and present together in a climax of meaning. Yosemite was never more beautiful than when John Muir leapt its peaks and gazed upon it with love and delight.

6. *Baptism*

During his second summer in Yosemite John Muir worked guiding tourists as well as operating a sawmill. Along the rough roads traveled stagecoach loads of tourists, breathing the dust raised by the horses. Like the domestic sheep driven to the mountains to graze, they were not miraculously transformed into free mountain sheep when exposed to the domes and waterfalls of Yosemite. Awed, entertained, and exhausted, they left the same people as they came. Few were born over again.

Muir would devote much of his life to the challenge of interpreting the wild to the men and women of civil society. Though few have done it so well, he found it a discouraging task. For one thing, interpreting nature took attention away from the truly important work of "gaping" at the wilderness.

> Instead of narrowing my attention to bookmaking out of material I have already eaten and drunken, I would rather stand in what all the world would call an idle manner, literally gaping with all the mouths of soul and body, demanding nothing, fearing nothing, but hoping and enjoying enormously. So-called sentimental, transcendental dreaming seems the only sensible and substantial business that one can engage in.[1]

Then there was the problem of how, in fact, one could help civilized people open their sensibilities to nature. Muir's experiences as a guide convinced him that the distance between the splendors of Yosemite and the sensibility of most tourists—even the well-meaning among them—was simply too great. The views and spectacles were overwhelming; "the inexperienced observer is oppressed by the incomprehensible grandeur."[2] Human feelings of alienation from nature, rather than being lessened by Yosemite, were reenforced by the valley's magnificence.

In April 1872 the *Overland Monthly* published "Twenty Hill Hollow," one of Muir's first attempts to prepare tourists to visit Yosemite and the High Sierra.[3] Of all Muir's essays, this may exhibit the greatest psychological and spiritual discernment—though it was unlikely many would follow his prescription.

Muir noted the horde who "make a trial of their speed" to race to Yosemite in season. Among these he addressed himself to "the few travelers who are in earnest—true lovers of the truth and beauty of wildness." He urged them to linger in a simpler valley among the Sierra foothills so they might learn how to experience nature and thus prepare themselves for Yosemite. The valley he selected, Twenty Hill Hollow, was one where he had grazed sheep his first winter in California, before he himself had climbed to the Sierra peaks.

> This delightful Hollow is less than a mile in length, and of just sufficient width to form a well-proportioned oval. . . . Here is no towering dome, no Tissiak, to mark its place; and one may ramble close upon its rim before he is made aware of its existence. Its twenty hills are as wonderfully regular in size and position as in form. They are like big marbles half buried in the ground, each poised and settled daintily into its place at a regular distance from its fellows, making a charming fairy-land of hills, with small, grassy valleys between, each valley having a tiny stream of its own, which leaps and sparkles out into the open hollow, uniting to form Hollow Creek.

This valley presented beauty on a human scale. "[O]ur moderate arithmetical standards are not outraged by a single magnitude of this simple, comprehensible hollow."

"The Hollow is not rich in birds," Muir recorded. Indeed there was only one, the meadowlark, whose song appealed to most people. Muir took time to describe three distinct sounds he had heard the lark make, so the visitor would be alert to them. Then, in his first ecology lesson, Muir noted that the hollow was indeed filled with sounds delightful in themselves, even if few appealed to humans.

> ... this song of the blessed lark [is] universally absorbable by human souls. It seems to be the only bird-song of these hills that has been created with any direct reference to us. Music is one of the attributes of matter, into whatever forms it may be organized ... but our senses are not fine enough to catch the tones. Fancy the waving, pulsing melody of the vast flower-congregations of the Hollow flowing from myriad voices of tuned petal and pistil, and heaps of sculptured pollen. Scarce one note is for us; nevertheless, God be thanked for this blessed instrument hid beneath the feathers of a lark.

Of animals, the antelope had been driven away and the hare now dominated. Muir lingered on the coyote, "beautiful and graceful in motion, with erect ears, and a bushy tail, like a fox," because it also was threatened, "cordially detested by 'sheep-men.' " And the ground squirrel too was "accursed" by humans, "because of his relish for grain. What a pity that Nature should have made so many small mouths palated like our own!" Yet Muir quickly left this gentle social criticism to return to stimulating the visitor's sensibility. He had a larger goal in view.

Carefully leading his readers' attention, Muir dwelt on the incredible display of wildflowers which followed the winter rains and reached its peak in March and April.

> Count the flowers of any portion of these twenty hills, or of the bottom of the Hollow, among the streams: you will find that there are from one to ten thousand upon every square yard. ... One would fancy that these California days receive more gold from the ground than they give to it. The earth has indeed become a sky; and the two cloudless skies, raying toward each other flower-beams and sunbeams, are fused and congolded into one glowing heaven.

Like a skilled revival preacher who had brought his audience to see the gates of heaven, Muir then made a vigorous plea for conversion.

If you wish to see a plant-resurrection,—myriads of bright flowers crowding from the ground, like souls to a judgment,—go to
Twenty Hills. . . . If you are traveling for health, play truant to
doctors and friends, fill your pocket with biscuits, and hide in
the hills of the Hollow, lave in its waters, tan in its golds, bask
in its flower-shine, and your baptisms will make you a new
creature indeed. Or, choked in the sediments of society, so tired
of the world, here will your hard doubts disappear, your carnal
incrustations melt off, and your soul breathe deep and free in
God's shoreless atmosphere of beauty and love.

"John Baptist" was in full form. He was not just interpreting. His aim was conversion. He wished to lead men and women
to a natural environment they might appreciate without fear and
then immerse them in it so they might emerge new creatures.
Muir followed the call to baptism with his personal testimony.
"Never shall I forget my baptism in this font. It happened in January, a resurrection day for many a plant and for me."

Muir ended his appeal with a quiet word to the circle of
those who he imagined had emerged from the baptism as new
creatures. The alienation of persons and nature had been overcome. No more would the new persons require a shelter, a bar-
rier to separate them from the living world. Now they were at
home in Twenty Hill Hollow. No longer vulnerable or defen-
sive, the visitors felt their senses opened; they fully experienced the hills, the sun, and the flowers. Muir knew the
sensation well: "You bathe in these spirit-beams, turning
round and round, as if warming at a camp-fire. Presently you
lose consciousness of your own separate existence: you blend
with the landscape, and become part and parcel of nature."

Muir then invited his converts to follow their baptismal
immersion in these gentle hills with communion at a higher
altar: "What have mountains fifty or a hundred miles away to
do with Twenty Hill Hollow?" The High Sierra themselves
might now slowly approach these renewed men and women, not
overwhelming them but entering their consciousness spiritually "as a circle of friends."

Muir found a vocation in the effort to help men and
women from the cities overcome their sense of alienation from

nature and develop a new relationship. Since this alienation was part of the fabric of urban, industrial, exploitative society, the change required a new birth. However it might distract him from his personal communion with Yosemite, Muir heard the call to be not just an interpreter of wilderness, but a prophet, a "John Baptist."

* * *

John Muir was a gentle, tolerant evangelist. He did not create a wilderness sect or insist that each person experience a change of heart and an opening of senses before being allowed in Yosemite. As a young man he had learned to despise sectarianism. "I do not like the doctrine of close[d] communion as held by hard shells," he wrote to his brother in 1870, "because the whole clumsy structure . . . rests upon a foundation of coarse-grained dogmatism. . . . [E]xclusiveness upon any subject is hateful, but it becomes absolutely hideous and impious in matters of religion."[4]

On the other hand, he was serious. He was a radical, not just a romantic. He knew that people were trapped, economically and spiritually, in the life-destroying drudgeries of urban industrial life, and that part of their entrapment was fear of nature, fear that they could not survive beyond the familiar supports of house, street, store, and job. In one newspaper essay aimed not just at the cultivated but at the laborer, Muir broke off a discussion of bees to speak his heart to "all the overworked and defrauded toilers of California towns":

> There is no daylight in towns, and the weary public ought to know that there is light here, and I for one clear my skirts from the responsibility of silence by shouting a cordial *come*. . . . Come all who need rest and light, bending and breaking with over work, leave your profits and losses and metallic dividends and come. . . . [5]

* * *

Entering the wilderness, the new believers needed more eyes to see with than their own, more senses than the human to develop a full experience of the place. Muir developed his own version of an aid common among primitive peoples: he chose favorite animals through whom he deepened his experience of the wilderness environment. In his essays he helped readers see through the eyes of these creatures and feel the wilderness through their experience. Three such *totem* creatures were the Douglas squirrel, the water ouzel, and the mountain sheep.

Douglas Squirrel insured the fertility of the Sierra forest, as he moved among the branches: "Probably over fifty per cent of all the cones ripened on the Sierra are cut off and handled by the Douglas alone, and of those of the Big Trees [sequoia] perhaps ninety per cent pass through his hands."[6] Early in his Yosemite days Muir's eagerness to enter into the experience of this animal was acute. When Muir wrote Jeanne Carr of his ecstasy beneath the sequoia, quoted earlier, he wrote also of his desire to digest the squirrel like communion bread, that he might somehow enter into the squirrel's fellowship with the trees.

> Come Suck Sequoia & be saved. Douglass Squirrel is so pervaded with rosin & burr juice his flesh can scarce be eaten even by mountaineers. No wonder he is so charged with magnetism. One of the little lions ran across my feet the other day as I lay resting under a fir & the effect was a thrill like a battery shock, I would eat him no matter how rosiny for the lightening he holds. I wish I could eat wilder things. . . . There goes Squirrel Douglass the master spirit of the tree top. It has just occurred to me how his belly is buffy brown, his back silver-gray. Ever since the first Adam of his race saw trees & burrs, his belly has been rubbing upon buff bark, & his back has been combed with silvery needles. Would that some of you wise—terribly wise Social scientists might discover some method of living as true to nature as the buff people of the woods running as free as the winds & waters among the burrs & filbert thickets of these leafy mothery woods.[7]

In his many essays on the Sierra forests and trees, Muir often used the squirrel's eyes, senses, and movements to help the reader experience forest ecology. He succeeded in establishing communion with Douglas Squirrel. The characteristics of the two — squirrel and Muir — became similar. "[T]he Douglass . . . leaps and glides in hidden strength, seemingly as independent of common muscles as a mountain stream . . . getting into what seem to be the most impossible situations without sense of danger. . . . He is, without exception, the wildest animal I ever saw."[8]

Once, like Francis of Assisi, Muir entertained a congregation of squirrels, along with chipmunks and birds, who gathered attentively as he sang and whistled Scottish airs: "Bonnie Doon," "Lass o' Gowrie," "O'er the Water to Charlie," "Bonnie Woods o' Cragie Lee," and others. Here was happy communion indeed! But when he began the Calvinist hymn "Old Hundredth," the squirrels fled. "What there can be in that grand old church-tune that is so offensive to birds and squirrels I can't imagine," Muir mused.[9] Perhaps Muir's tone was less confident and joyful when he turned from songs of the Scottish hills to a song from the Scottish kirk. Squirrels may indeed have sensitivities humans do not anticipate.

* * *

In his journals Muir mentioned the water ouzel more frequently than any other creature. This small bird that fished the rapids was a constant, reliable companion.

> Among all the countless waterfalls I have met in the course of ten years' exploration in the Sierra, . . . not one was found without its Ouzel. No cañon is too cold for this little bird, none too lonely, provided it be rich in falling water. . . . Among all the mountain birds, none has cheered me so much in my lonely wanderings.[10]

Fully expressing Muir's joy in water, his desire to enter into the life and vitality of the mountain streams, the ouzel lived a perpetual, wild baptism.

> These rocks have not been stained by the foot of man. . . . Here is an ecstasy of water and wild melody. . . . One bird, the ouzel, loves this gorge and flies through it, merrily stopping to sing, not on the water's edge, but down on a boulder half buried in foam.[11]

The ouzel traveled singly, flying the streams Muir followed as he searched the paths of glaciers. "Were the flights of all the ouzels in the Sierra traced on a chart, they would indicate the direction of the flow of the entire system of ancient glaciers." They were such an intimate part of the stream, "one might almost be pardoned in fancying they come direct from the living waters, like flowers from the ground." The ouzels embodied communion with the waters. Their ever-cheerful song spoke of the Lord of the waters, "throughout the whole of their beautiful lives interpreting all that we in our unbelief call terrible in the utterances of torrents and storms, as only varied expressions of God's eternal love."[12]

I think of John Muir as a wild mountain sheep. Muir's own experience of mountain sheep, however, was more subtle than such simple identification. The mountain sheep represented a wild nobility which exceeded the human. Muir felt judged by them.

In September 1873, Muir had an opportunity to observe a flock of mountain sheep at length, some "making leaps on glacial bosses that made me hold my breath. . . . I could have scaled the same precipice, but not where they did."[13] He noted with approval their individuality, each able to find its own way. In an essay years later, he contrasted them with domestic sheep.

> . . . each one of the flock, while following the guidance of the most experienced, yet climbed with intelligent independence as a perfect individual, capable of separate existence whenever it should wish or be compelled to withdraw from the little clan. The domestic sheep, on the contrary, is only a fraction of an animal, a whole flock being required to form an individual.[14]

The following year Muir met some hunters near Mount Shasta, including "three from Bonnie Scotland." On impulse he joined their hunt for wild sheep, though he did not carry a weapon himself. Muir lingered behind during the first day's hunt. "It seems that some sixty or eighty head in different flocks were seen during the day, and a few patent bullets from three-hundred-dollar rifles scattered among them without effect." The second day a lamb was killed. On the third day Muir was present and observed one of his fellows shoot "a noble old ram" and then, seconds later, drop a ewe with his second barrel. "Well done Scotch rifle!" Muir exclaimed with native pride, and later noted that "the scene was wildly exciting." Muir then broke his written narrative to reflect on the pulsing of his own blood.

> Leading the mean, lean lives we do, we little know how much wildness there is in us. Only a few centuries separate us from great-grandfathers that were savage as wolves; this is the secret of our love for the hunt. Savageness is natural . . . . In the wild exhilaration raised by the running of the game, and the firing, and the pursuit of the wounded, we could have torn and worried like mastiffs, but all this passed away, and we were Christians again. We went up to the ewe . . . . She was still breathing, but helpless. Her eye was remarkably mild and gentle, and called out sympathy as if she were human. Poor woman-sheep![15]

I recall no other instance where Muir used "wildness" in a derogatory sense. He was shaken by his own blood-rush. Muir had urged us to let our feelings run free in the wild, but here he recognized that humans need not just to be natural, but to be Christians as well. We need an ecology, a morality, so we grasp "the truth and beauty of wildness."[16] Moral beauty, not blood-rush, should guide the expression of our feelings.

Muir admired the wild sheep, "the bravest of all the Sierra mountaineers."[17] He was glad their mountain knowledge and skills exceeded his. Their beauty reminded him of his sin, of moments when wildness parted from love. He did not feel he was a mountain sheep. Their character was beyond human grasp because, "like stars and angels, they dwell mostly above his reach in the sky."[18]

7. *Glacial Eye*

John Muir was rightly proud of his glacial eye. He was the first to see the impact of the glaciers in the formation of the Sierra, particularly Yosemite and the other great canyons. Though subsequent studies have corrected details of his analysis, his general perspective was confirmed. He took pride not only in his discoveries, but in the way he achieved them: rambling free, "gaping with all the mouths of soul and body," opening his senses to nature and reading its pages.

The religious implications of glaciation were as important to Muir as the scientific. He wished to correct a religious orientation which permeated his age. The rigorously pious, like his father, saw this world as a vale of suffering and a scene of struggle. This world was not to be loved but feared and endured in the hope of a better one to come. On the other hand the new Darwinians, optimistic about this world, also grounded their optimism in a sense of conflict. The struggles of evolution were yielding the fittest—the strong among the human race—to rule the rest of nature.

Within his glacial perspective Muir sensed beauty and value in each stage of evolution. All were fit and none were lost. One stage, one species was not the goal of creation: all were, all are, and there are more to come. Placing his reader high above Yosemite on the shoulder of Mount Ritter, Muir wrote,

> Could we have been here to observe during the glacial period, we should have overlooked a wrinkled ocean of ice as continuous as that now covering the landscapes of Greenland; filling every valley and cañon with only the tops of the fountain peaks rising darkly above the rock-encumbered ice-waves like

islets in a stormy sea—those islets the only hints of the glorious landscapes now smiling in the sun. Standing here in the deep, brooding silence all the wilderness seems motionless, as if the work of creation were done. But in the midst of this outer stead-fastness we know there is incessant motion and change. Ever and anon, avalanches are falling from yonder peaks. These cliff-bound glaciers, seemingly wedged and immovable, are flowing like water and grinding the rocks beneath them. The lakes are lapping their granite shores and wearing them away, and every one of the these rills and young rivers is fretting the air into music, and carrying the mountains to the plains. Here are the roots of all the life of the valleys, and here more simply than elsewhere is the eternal flux of nature manifested. Ice changing to water, lakes to meadows, and mountains to plains. And while we thus contemplate Nature's methods of landscape creation, and, reading the records she has carved on the rocks, recon-struct, however imperfectly, the landscapes of the past, we also learn that as these we now behold have succeeded those of the pre-glacial age, so they in turn are withering and vanishing to be succeeded by others yet unborn.[1]

Muir proposed that we incorporate the history read in nature into our religious experience and memory. As he would lead us to enter a sensuous, trusting relation with wilderness, so he would teach us to honor nature's past and see the great "destructive" forces as part of God's loving creativity: "A mile away is a ridge of pre-glacial lava, the residual mass of fiery floods. . . . And over the meadows an avalanche of water, rocks, and logs swept a few years ago. . . . The cooled lava is forested now. The sun shines lovingly upon it, and all is joyous life." These are "Nature's modes of working towards beauty and joy." Glacier and volcano bring "landscapes, forests, and gardens with their tender loveliness."[2]

The Bible, stored in Muir's memory from childhood, includes depths not plumbed by the anxious otherworldliness of his father or by the excited anthropocentrism of the industrial era. There is the Genesis account of God's radiant delight in the formation of all species—"fresh growth, plants bearing seed according to their kind and trees bearing fruit each with seed according to its kind; and God saw that it was good" (Genesis 1:

12, NEB). There is God's rainbow covenant made not just with humans but with "every living creature" (Genesis 9:8-10, NEB); God's promise to protect the web of life and to draw all creatures into the history of salvation. There are psalms summoning all living things, along with rivers and hills, to praise God in confidence that God's judgment and care apply to them as well as to human society.

> Let the sea roar and all its creatures,
>   the world and those who dwell in it.
> Let the rivers clap their hands,
> let the hills sing aloud together
> before the LORD; for [God] comes
>   to judge the earth.
> [The LORD] will judge the world with righteousness
>   and the peoples in justice. (Psalm 98:7-9, NEB, alt.)

In the New Testament there is Jesus, attributing greater beauty to a field of flowers than to the regal decorations of King Solomon (Matthew 6:28; Luke 12:27, RSV). There is also Paul's promise that nature is not doomed to exploitation by wicked humanity but that "creation itself " may "obtain the glorious liberty of the children of God" (Romans 8:21, RSV). Whichever of these images Muir may have remembered, we are likely to recall them as we read Muir. The Bible does not exclude nature but draws nature into God's love, God's delight, and God's saving purpose.

Muir saw that part of the religious problem was integrating death into life. Life in this world is food chains, each drawing life from consuming other lives. We may improve our own religious understanding if, as we eat, we reflect on how the deaths of some contribute to the lives of others. Though abuse can make it so, this need not be a hostile process. Beneath its tensions an ecology nurtures life for all. Jesus' death, morally distinctive in its religious impact, participates in this life-giving ecology.

Muir urged us to experience natural history, to sense the past suffusing the present. "As a man in his books may be said to walk the world long after he is in his grave, so the glaciers flow again in their works—these stony books."[3] If we can read the past in the present, we bring life again to those who went before. We stretch ourselves beyond the boundaries of our own mortality.

> We read our Bibles and remain fearful and uncomfortable amid Nature's loving destructions, her beautiful deaths. Talk of immortality! After a whole day in the woods, we are already immortal. When is the end of such a day?[4]

Muir did not disparage the Christian hope of life beyond death. He did disparage those who cling to hope of future joy while closing themselves to the delights of the present. Life is awareness. If we hide from experience today, do we really wish more tomorrow, or beyond the grave? On the other hand, Muir thought those living in sensitive, spontaneous contact with their environment to be so filled with experience that they achieved a daily immortality. One day on the trail he jotted these thoughts after finding a dead bear:

> Civilized man chokes his soul as the heathen Chinese their feet. We deprecate bears.
>
> But grandly they blend with their native mountains. They roam the sandy slopes on lily meads, through polished glacier canyons, among the solemn firs and brown sequoia, manzanita, and chaparral, living upon red berries and gooseberries, little caring for rain or snow. . . . Magnificent bears of the Sierra are worthy of their magnificent homes. They are not companions of men, but children of God, and His charity is broad enough for bears. They are the objects of His tender keeping. . . .
>
> Bears are made of the same dust as we, and breathe the same winds and drink of the same waters. A bear's days are warmed by the same sun, his dwellings are overdomed by the same blue sky, and his life turns and ebbs with heart-pulsings like ours, and was poured from the same First Fountain. And whether he at last goes to our stingy heaven or no, he has terrestrial immortality. His life not long, not short, knows no beginning, no ending. To him life unstinted, unplanned, is above the accidents of time, and his years, markless and boundless, equal Eternity.
>
> God bless Yosemite bears![5]

Immortality has less to do with whether one is a person or a bear, than with one's awareness. "The kingdom of God," Jesus said, "is in the midst of you" (Luke 17:21, RSV).

Muir's glacial eye saw natural history, each page of which had beauty and value. Just as the beauty of each flower or tree is enhanced when one senses its ecological context—those from which it receives and to which it contributes—so also the beauty of each historical age or incident is enhanced by the recognition of its ancient origins and subsequent fruit. From this perspective we can see beauty even in the action of the avalanche.

Human history, then, nestles within a larger historical context, the history of nature. This perspective takes getting used to. We are more accustomed to thinking of history as human events, with nature as mere backdrop to the human play or raw material for human creativity. However, if nature has value, then it is urgent that we develop a sense of the relationships between natural and human history. In 1875, as Muir knew his time to leave was drawing near, he caressed Yosemite like a lover. "Every sense is satisfied," he wrote. "For us there is no past, no future—we live only in the present and are full." Yet a few sentences later he pondered age-old questions.

> I often wonder what men will do with the mountains. . . . Will a better civilization come, in accord with obvious nature, and all this wild beauty be set to human poetry? Another outpouring of lava or the coming of the glacial period could scarce wipe out the flowers and flowering shrubs more effectively than do the [herds of domestic] sheep. And what then is coming—what is the human part of the mountain's destiny?[6]

Years before, he had comforted himself with a very long perspective. When he rejected humanocentrism during his long walk to the Gulf, Muir had written, "After human beings have also played their part in Creation's plan, they too may disappear without any general burning or extraordinary commotion whatever."[7] Now, however, he knew the relationship was more complex than that. Human history and natural history are deeply, inextricably, intertwined. In this relationship the possibility of poetry is shadowed by the evidence of destruction.

The trooping of domestic sheep—"hoofed locusts," he liked to call them—was not truly the equivalent of a lava flood. Muir saw a volcanic eruption as a creative, purposeful act from the hand of God, whereas flocks of sheep in the High Sierra were a thoughtless, human intrusion, with no creative potential.

On the other hand, in communion with nature Muir knew the excitement of creativity. The earth is young. Muir proclaimed, "In the Divine Calender this is still the morning of Creation."[8]

> The last days of this glacial winter are not yet past; we live in "creation's dawn." The morning stars still sing together, and the world, though made, is still being made and becoming more beautiful every day.[9]

The world was becoming more beautiful every day, in this subjective appraisal, because Muir was seeing and feeling it more deeply. Here is the possibility of poetry which might enrich nature while redeeming us. Humanity is not simply irrelevant to nature's purpose, nor only a threat to its vitality. We are part of the ecology of this era. If sensitive and perceptive, we may join the creativity and contribute to natural life. When people are attuned to nature, our gifts of perception and reflection become part of the ecology, bringing its beauty to self-consciousness. This is poetry indeed. Here is the distinctive human vocation in the sweep of natural history. Here is the image of God: humanity, aware of creative relationships, expressing God's delight in nature.[10]

Feeling the tension between the human potential and the human threat, Muir knew he must do two things. One was to continue "gaping with all the mouths of soul and body," so he and wilderness might nourish each other. The other was to come down from the mountain and preach his gospel, announcing the new life available to those who would open themselves to nature. We need to be born over again, for our sake and for the sake of nature.

8. *Prophecy*

In 1874 Muir spent a ten-month "exile" in the Bay area—
marveling that "there is not a perfectly sane man in San Francisco"[1]—and then fled back to Yosemite. Yet hiding among
these beloved mountains could no longer be his destiny either.
"No one of the rocks seems to call me now, nor any of the distant
mountains. Surely this Merced and Tuolumne chapter of my
life is done. . . . I will not try [to] tell the Valley. Yet I feel that I
am a stranger here."[2] In a few weeks he felt more self-assured
and understood his calling again, declaring, "I am hopelessly
and forever a mountaineer. . . . I care to live only to entice people to look at Nature's loveliness."[3] At age thirty-six Muir
began fifteen years of uncertain striving to develop his vocation
as spokesman for wilderness. These years were his most difficult journey.

Despite his shyness in society and devotion to the mountains, Muir did not meet all his needs by wilderness. He cultivated many friendships through correspondence and joyfully
received visitors. His deepest relationship was with Jeanne
Carr, wife of his geology professor in Wisconsin, who sensed
from the beginning Muir's genius for experiencing nature and
encouraged him in his wanderings. Their forty-year correspondence includes Muir's most passionate expressions about
nature, shared with a woman he loved and trusted. The Carrs
moved to California during Muir's Yosemite years, and the
friends visited frequently. Jeanne arranged Muir's first publi-
cations. She continually urged him to write and to engage with
society, and later she introduced Muir to the woman he would
eventually marry. Both knew their love for each other was

deep, but Jeanne was married to another. Although they had
several opportunities to live under the same roof, each time one
or the other backed away.

Two other women fell in love with Muir during his
Yosemite years: the wife of his employer in the valley, and a
visiting novelist. Muir needed such affection, but he was
upright and feared the confining bonds of marriage. There is no
indication that any of these relationships were expressed sexu-
ally. Muir would likely have retreated quickly from such
expression, wary of its implications.[4]

In 1879 Muir proposed marriage to Louie Strentzel, a
quiet, stable homebody, the daughter of the leading fruit
rancher in California's Alhambra Valley. Immediately after
their engagement he left her waiting anxiously while he under-
took his first expedition to explore Alaska's glaciers. The couple
were married in April 1880, and later that summer Muir left
for Alaska again. These absences were hard on Louie. During
the years when Muir stayed home and compulsively attacked
the problems of the fruit ranch, however, she discovered that
confinement was even harder on him. By 1889, with the ranch
prosperous, two beloved daughters flourishing, and Muir himself languishing, Louie urged her husband to resume his exploration and writing. She faithfully backed him during the
remaining sixteen years of her life when he was often away
exploring a wilderness or speaking to urban audiences.

* * *

When he descended from the mountains, Muir's principal
challenge was to find his voice. We who now read his journals
and letters know what an evocative voice Muir had, how beau-
tifully he conveyed his immediate experience. But when he
imagined his audience, his confidence shriveled. He was sensitive that words could not substitute for experience itself.

> I have a low opinion of books; they are but piles of stones set
> up to show coming travelers where other minds have been, or at
> best signal smokes to call attention.... No amount of word-
> making will ever make a single soul to *know* these mountains.

> As well seek to warm the naked and frostbitten by lectures on caloric and pictures of flame. One day's exposure to mountains is better than cartloads of books.[5]

When Muir began to write for publication, he felt intimidated by literary expectations. In the nineteenth century, literature was a solemn cultural enterprise. Great writers like Emerson and Thoreau had worked hard at their craft, and the field was littered with aesthetic conventions. Writing for publication was "work." When Muir approached work, he became a compulsive perfectionist. So he labored over his writing, unable to start, revising repeatedly, complaining constantly. He afflicted himself with impossible standards. "It is so difficult . . . to make the meaning stand out through the words like a fire on a hill so that all must see it without looking for it. Yet this is what the times demand in magazine work."[6]

> I never can tell how anything I begin of a literary kind will end. Sometimes my descriptions are contemptibly mean and lean and scrawny, without any color or atmosphere about them, again they are all fluffily sentimentous drifting about unguided and foundationless as mist, too thin for any terrestrial use. . . . To write to order and measure I am about the worst hand you could find.[7]

The literary techniques Muir developed were magnificent. He took the reader with him into the wilderness, helping the reader see nature through the eyes of other creatures. In Muir's writings education was tucked under the cover of event, and mere intellectual response gave way to empathy. God was introduced through natural sacraments, yet this God was recognizable to the churchgoer. Though Muir was always happy to scribble in his journal, the growing public admiration did not help him enjoy the task of writing for publication. To the end of his life he treated writing as a painful necessity. He proclaimed with Aaron's tongue, but he complained like Moses.

Muir also approached public speaking anxiously. Once launched, however, feeling the audience's response to his stories, he would relax and glow with enthusiasm. He became a popular speaker before audiences in the east as well as the west and was even more engaging at informal gatherings, telling stories to friends. Sometimes, to their delight, he told his daughters serial stories which would last for days.

Best of all, though, was John Muir introducing a friend firsthand to the wilderness. Then he was all animation, supplying nonstop commentary and history, racing ahead and urging his footsore companion to follow, yet so engaging that few who shared this experience failed to treasure it as a high moment of life. Often those who walked with Muir in the wilderness returned converted, their eyes opened, caring for this landscape and dedicated to its protection.

* * *

John Muir was fifty-one years old in 1889 when his prophetic career began in earnest. Robert Underwood Johnson, editor of the influential *Century* magazine, came to California that year to meet Muir and find out if he was willing to write again after several years' farming. Muir was ready to flee the fruit trees. He took the man to Yosemite, where Johnson felt the impact of both the landscape and his guide.

The valley was still a poorly managed state park, while the surrounding highlands, totally unprotected, were showing the ravages of sheep grazing. When Muir deplored the impact of these "hoofed locusts," Johnson observed that the solution was to create a national park encompassing the highlands surrounding the state park in Yosemite valley. Yellowstone National Park, established in 1872, was a precedent. Before the two left the high country they struck a bargain. Muir would write two articles for *Century* describing the beauties of Yosemite and the dangers of neglect and recommending boundaries for a national park. Johnson would use the articles to lobby Congress for park legislation.

Muir's articles were published in 1890, Johnson lobbied skillfully, and legislation sailed through Congress, creating a large park with the boundaries Muir recommended. It included the Mariposa Grove of giant sequoia to the south of the Yosemite, the Hetch Hetchy canyon to the north, and the tributary highlands surrounding both valleys. The bill quickly became law under the signature of President William Henry Harrison. The victory, won swiftly in the east before California sheep ranchers had time to organize opposition, was unrealistically easy.

Muir's friends in San Francisco now felt it important to form an association to defend the new park against an anticipated reaction and to influence its management. In May 1892, the Sierra Club was organized with John Muir as president. "I had never seen Mr. Muir so animated and happy before," a friend recalled. "In the Sierra Club he saw the crystallization of the dreams and labor of a lifetime."[8] Immediately the club began working to get underbrush cleared in the valley and to oppose a new bill in Congress which aimed at reducing the national park's boundaries.

The club continued meeting in San Francisco, but participation dwindled until a concerned lawyer, William Colby, organized a Yosemite outing for July 1901, which Muir promised to attend. A hundred members camped out for a month, exploring the park and listening to Muir in the evenings. "God's ozone sparkles in every eye," Muir wrote Louie. "I never before saw so big and merry a camp circle, a huge fire blazing in the center. I had, of course, to make a little speech."[9] Similar outings were repeated in subsequent summers. Thus the pattern was established for the distinctive Sierra Club vitality, combining group mountain adventures with political action to defend wilderness.

In 1896 the Grover Cleveland administration appointed a Forestry Commission to appraise the condition of western forests. The government still owned, but did not regulate, millions of acres of timber. They were freely plundered by settlers, loggers, railroads, and mining interests. Gifford Pinchot, the nation's only trained forester, was appointed secretary to the commission, and John Muir, now the popular voice of America's wilderness, was invited to tour with the commission *ex officio*. Following the commission's recommendations, President Cleveland set aside twenty-one million acres of forest reserves.

This act touched off a decade of intense public debate and congressional maneuvering over the extent of national forest reserves and how they should be managed.

Muir's participation in this debate showed the matured prophet at his finest. He had developed an ecological populism. The pressing need he saw was for ordinary people—whose interest was beauty, not profit—to visit the remaining forests and wildernesses. They would defend "God's trees." Muir believed that abuses "are done in the darkness of ignorance and unbelief, for when light comes, the heart of the people is always right."[10]

> The regular tourist, ever on the flow, is one of the most characteristic productions of the present century; and however frivolous and inappreciative the poorest specimens may appear, viewed comprehensively, they are a most hopeful and significant sign of the time, indicating at least the beginning of our return to nature, for going to the mountains is going home.[11]

Writing for eager audiences about "The Wild Parks and Forest Reservations of the West," Muir rang out the invitation. "Thousands of tired, nerve-shaken, over-civilized people are beginning to find out that going to the mountains is going home; that wildness is a necessity; and that mountain parks and reservations are useful not only as fountains of timber and irrigating rivers, but as fountains of life." Time spent in the wild will enhance your life, he professed: "Give a month at least to this precious reserve. The time will not be taken from the sum of your life. Instead of shortening, it will indefinitely lengthen it and make you truly immortal." Muir reassured his urban readers that these strange places were safe. "No American wilderness that I know of is so dangerous as a city home 'with all the modern improvements.' One should go to the woods for safety, if for nothing else."[12]

Gifford Pinchot, the European-trained professional, defended government forest reserves on grounds of economic utility. Government ownership would assure orderly, sustainable use. "The first principle of conservation is development," he asserted and urged the nation to manage these reserves to achieve the greatest economic yield.[13]

Muir disagreed, arguing that forests embody a broad range of values. "The forests of America, however slighted by man, must have been a great delight to God; for they were the best he ever planted." Muir eloquently insisted that tall trees are not just erect lumber; they are spiritual, "lordly monarchs proclaiming the gospel of beauty like apostles." The pace of logging, he continued, was both economically and spiritually destructive. "Clearing has surely now gone far enough; soon timber will be scarce, and not a grove will be left to rest in or pray in." Sound forest management, Muir emphasized, should limit cutting to methods which protect both the beauty and the ecological health of a forest.

> In their natural condition, or under wise mangement, keeping out destructive sheep, preventing fires, selecting the trees that should be cut for lumber, and preserving the young ones and the shrubs and sod of herbaceous vegetation, these forests would be a never failing fountain of wealth and beauty.[14]

All sentimentality laid aside, Muir addressed some hard economic and political issues which utilitarian conservationists habitually ignored. He noted that much more timber was burned by arson or cut and left rotting on the ground than was used for lumber. "Every mill is a centre of destruction far more severe from waste and fire than from use." The railroads were particularly culpable. When they cleared rights-of-way, they often did not clean the fallen wood back a safe distance from the track. Sparks from locomotives ignited these brush piles, and the wind whipped the fires into the forests.

> The half-dozen transcontinental railroad companies advertise the beauties of their lines. ... [Yet] every train rolls on through dismal smoke and barbarous, melancholy ruins; and the companies might well cry in their advertisements: "Come! travel our way. Ours is the blackest."[15]

Muir saw capitalism run amuck in the western forests. Small, unregulated lumbermen had done damage, but now these were being undersold by giant mills which also stole from public forests, employing gangs of temporary squatters to lay fraudulent claims. "By such methods," Muir lamented, "have our magnificent redwoods and much of the sugar-pine forests of the Sierra Nevada been absorbed by foreign and resident capitalists."[16] Muir appealed to the small lumberman to support federal controls which would break these monopolies while regulating and protecting individual access. Indeed, Muir urged homesteading families to settle near properly regulated forests and use them, as an alternative to industrial lumbering. "Good men of every nation, seeking freedom and homes and bread" should be welcome.

> Every place is made better by them. . . . The ground will be glad to feed them, and the pines will come down from the mountains for their homes . . .willingly. . . . Nor will the woods be the worse for this use, or their benign influences be diminished any more than the sun is diminished by shining. Mere destroyers, however, tree-killers, wool and mutton men, spreading death and confusion in the fairest groves and gardens ever planted,— let the government hasten to cast them out and make an end of them.[17]

Every American should have access to wild nature, for his and her spiritual benefit, and for the sake of the forest itself. "If every citizen could take one walk through this reserve, there would be no more trouble about its care; for only in darkness does vandalism flourish."[18]

*   *   *

In 1903 Muir, at sixty-five, enjoyed what were surely the most satisfying days of his prophetic career. The president, Theodore Roosevelt, asked Muir to guide him personally through Yosemite. "I do not want anyone with me but you, and I want to drop politics absolutely for four days and just be out in the open with you." Suspecting that Muir would use the occasion to lobby for transfer of Yosemite valley to federal jurisdiction, a group of California politicians tried to sabotage the outing. They set up an alternative banquet for the president at a hotel in Wawona, near the Mariposa Grove of giant sequoia, and diverted the presidential luggage to their hotel.

> After seeing the grove that afternoon, TR asked for his suitcase. By a suspicious accident, it had been sent on to Wawona. The President's jaw snapped shut. *"Get it!"* he said. ("Never did I hear two words spoken so much like bullets," Muir later recalled.) The suitcase was retrieved. On horseback, with a cook and two packers, Muir and Roosevelt set forth by themselves.

> Muir made him a bed of crisscrossed evergreen boughs. "It was clear weather, and we lay in the open," Roosevelt noted, "the enormous cinnamon-colored trunks rising above us like the columns of a vaster and more beautiful cathedral than was ever conceived by any human architect."[19]

Muir and Roosevelt deeply impressed each other. They awoke one morning buried in snow, and another evening they had to dodge a banquet interception in Yosemite valley; but they completed their trip together and parted reluctantly. Roosevelt promised to extend federal forest protection up the High Sierra from Yosemite to Mount Shasta near the Oregon border. Furthermore, he vowed to sign a bill for the Yosemite valley if one reached his desk.

Muir then launched a campaign to persuade the California legislature to return the Yosemite valley to the federal government. Railroad and stagecoach interests had stood in the way, but Muir's friend E. H. Harriman took control of the Southern Pacific Railroad, and that tipped the balance. In 1905 the California legislature approved the bill, and in 1906 President Roosevelt signed the federal law incorporating the valley into Yosemite National Park.

Theodore Roosevelt remains the outstanding conservationist president in America's history. He harnessed the preservationist vision that John Muir had nurtured among a growing segment of the American public, and he also gathered behind him the utilitarian conservationists exemplified by Gifford Pinchot, whom he appointed to head a new United States Forest Service. To both these streams of energy he added his own driving commitment.

Roosevelt stretched politics as far as he could to protect America's remaining preserves of unspoiled nature. He created five new national parks, sixteen national monuments, and fifty-three wildlife reserves. Congress responded by trying to block the creation of additional forest reserves in six western states without its legislative consent. Before signing this bill into law, Roosevelt created or enlarged thirty-two reserves totaling seventy-five million acres, doubling the forest areas under federal protection. He justified this extravagant act with populist sentiments similar to those Muir had expressed: he was merely protecting the rights of potential settlers against "the lumber syndicates."[20]

*   *   *

San Francisco needed a better source for municipal water. In 1901 city representatives slipped a bill through Congress allowing water conduits through national parks for public and beneficial uses. Then the city applied to the Interior Department to build a dam across the mouth of Hetch Hetchy valley within Yosemite National Park. The Sierra Club and other friends of Yosemite had been caught sleeping.

At first the Interior Department refused. But after the crippling San Francisco earthquake and fire in 1907, the needs of this growing city for water became an appealing national concern. Within the Roosevelt administration, Gifford Pinchot, willing to allow national parks to be exploited for economic benefit, argued that Hetch Hetchy might be dammed with no aesthetic loss. In San Francisco even some Sierra Club members supported the municipal proposal. Those who opposed it seemed to be placing sentimental aesthetics ahead of evident human need.

In fact, the Hetch Hetchy valley within the park was only one of several sites which could have provided the water. The particular attraction of this site was that there a dam could be high enough to generate electricity. Though the city emphasized only its desire for water, it pursued this particular site in the hope of cheap municipal power as well.

John Muir could not have felt greater anguish if his own child were on the auction block. "Dam Hetch Hetchy! As well dam for water-tanks the people's cathedrals and churches, for no holier temple has ever been consecrated by the heart of man."[21] The Hetch Hetchy valley was a geological sister to Yosemite, comparable in size, with spectacular scenic features of its own. Fed by the Tuolumne River after it passed through the beautiful Tuolumne meadows, Hetch Hetchy was part of Muir's first explorations. It was part of his first Yosemite love; he had obtained its inclusion in the national park.

When he took pen to defend Hetch Hetchy, Muir placed his readers right in the valley, on a spot which might soon be under water and inaccessible.

> Lowlanders are apt to suppose that mountain streams in their wild career over cliffs lose control of themselves and tumble in a noisy chaos of mist and spray. On the contrary, on no part of their travels are they more harmonious and self-controlled. Imagine yourself in Hetch Hetchy on a sunny day in June, standing waist-deep in grass and flowers (as I have often stood), while the great pines sway dreamily with scarcely perceptible motion. Looking northward across the Valley you see a plain, gray granite cliff rising abruptly out of the gardens and groves to a height of 1800 feet, and in front of it Tueeulala's [the falls'] silvery scarf burning with irised sun-fire. In the first white outburst at the head there is abundance of visible energy, but it is speedily hushed and concealed in divine repose, and its tranquil progress to the base of the cliff is like that of a downy feather in a still room. Now observe the fineness and marvelous distinctness of the various sun-illumined fabrics into which the water is woven; they sift and float from form to form down the face of that grand gray rock in so leisurely and unconfused a manner that you can examine their texture, and patterns and tones of color as you would a piece of embroidery held in the hand. Toward the top of the fall you see groups of blooming, comet-like masses, their solid, white heads separate, their tails like combed silk interlacing among delicate gray and purple shadows, ever forming and dissolving, worn out by friction in their rush through the air. Most of these vanish in a few hundred feet below the summit, changing to varied forms of cloud-like drapery. Near the bottom the width of the fall has increased from about twenty-five feet to a hundred feet. Here it is com-

posed of yet finer tissues, and is still without a trace of disor-
der—air, water and sunlight woven into stuff that spirits might
wear.

So fine a fall might well seem sufficient to glorify any valley; but here, as in Yosemite, Nature seems in nowise moderate,
for a short distance to the eastward of Tueeulala booms and
thunders the great Hetch Hetchy Fall, Wapama, so near that
you have both of them in full view from the same standpoint.

Muir also responded to the practical arguments. Sub-
merging the Hetch Hetchy valley in 175 feet of water would
not, as some claimed, "enhance its beauty by forming a crystal-
clear lake." Like the mountain snows, the lake would be sea-
sonal. Much of the year it would be bordered by sterile shores
and vast mud flats. The water would not be distinctively pure
for drinking, as claimed, but polluted by heavy tourist use of
the Tuolumne meadows upstream. Flooding Hetch Hetchy valley would reduce by one-third the number of tourists who could
camp uncrowded in Yosemite Park. For a little cheap electricity, this was an uneconomic as well as an unaesthetic
exchange.

Muir was right on every point. Hetch Hetchy reservoir
today is a neglected eyesore in the midst of vast beauty, while
visitors critically overcrowd the Yosemite valley. But Muir and
the Sierra Club had failed to make Hetch Hetchy a tourist
attraction, popularizing it by its own name prior to the crisis.
Incorporating Hetch Hetchy into the park had been too easy.
Despite its magnificence, few people were personally attached
to it. Now when San Francisco pressed its own emotional
appeal, those conservationists who claimed to be most rational
capitulated, and Muir was left looking like an isolated nature-
fanatic. Indeed the old man, now a widower, was often testy
during this long battle in which even his friends were divided.
In December 1913, Congress approved San Francisco's request
and President Woodrow Wilson signed the law.

Angry but resigned, Muir expressed the hope that "in
spite of Satan & Co. some sort of compensation must surely
come out of this dark dam- dam- damnation."[22] It did. The com-

pensation was a necessary lesson which environmentalists, Muir's spiritual children, have learned and remembered. No wild place is secure without continued watchfulness, and no wild place is safe without a public which knows it and cares for it. It is not enough to be reasonable conservationists; people need to experience the earth, and to love it. Nor is it enough for a wild place to be left alone. For its survival in the modern world, every landscape needs lovers.

9. *Agriculture*

Creating parks and reserves to protect the wild is a critical part of relating responsibly to the earth. There need to be environments where humanity does not alter the ecology, and there need to be places where humans may experience the wild. Across most of the earth, however, human culture has a profound impact upon natural life. Indeed, the basic systems of life-support on this planet—the quality of air and water, fundamental chemical and organic interactions—are now vulnerable to human impact. Humanity and the rest of nature must achieve productive, interactive relationships. Before ending my dialogue with John Muir, I want to think with him about these relationships: not just farming, but the ways human culture relates to the earth—*agri-culture* in a broad sense.

Muir's personal experience with farming was not edifying. Homesteading, as practiced by his father and many of their Wisconsin neighbors, was grim exploitation of land, livestock, and children. At age eleven young John was clearing trees and brush from the virgin earth, setting giant bonfires which his father instructively compared to the flames of hell. The next spring he was driving oxen from dawn to dusk, wrestling a huge plow through the clods and tangled roots. He watched his father work the family horse to death, and he himself received regular beatings that were "outrageously severe." After wasting the abundant timber, the family shivered around a meager stove. There is a suggestion that Daniel Muir ordered his son to steal timber from nearby government land. Seven crop years later, the soil of the original homestead was exhausted, and Daniel moved his family to another where the clearing cycle began again. This time, however, all the work fell to John, his

younger brother, and the girls. His father supervised, read
Scripture, and—to the relief of his family—left occasionally for
preaching itinerations.

Though he despised farm life, Muir recalled with delight
"that glorious Wisconsin wilderness" of his childhood. Here, in
moments snatched from work and on the blessed sabbath, he
explored the rich environment upon which the homesteads
were encroaching. Young John did not identify with the human
vocation of agriculture but with free, wild nature which, like
himself, was abused and subdued.[1]

When Muir reached the Yosemite area his first job was
tending sheep. He was appalled to discover that human ingenu-
ity had bred a creature which rivaled the homesteader in
destructiveness. "As sheep advance, flowers, vegetation, grass,
soil, plenty, and poetry vanish."[2] On the other hand nature, left
to her own devices, produced abundance without such woeful
side effects. This too was amazing. Muir puzzled, "I have often
tried to understand how so many deer, and wild sheep, and
bears, and flocks of grouse—nature's cattle and poultry—could
be allowed to run at large through the mountain gardens without in any way marring their beauty."[3] As he came to know
mountain sheep, Muir realized how far the domestic had fallen
from its progenitors.

> . . . we may observe that the domestic sheep, in a general way, is
> expressionless, like a dull bundle of something only half alive,
> while the wild is as elegant and graceful as a deer, every move-
> ment manifesting admirable strength and character. The tame
> is timid; the wild is bold. The tame is always more or less ruf-
> fled and dirty; while the wild is as smooth and clean as the flow-
> ers of his mountain pastures.[4]

During that fateful hunt on Mount Shasta with his Scottish companions, Muir discovered more than chagrin at the
rush of his own blood-lust. He examined closely the carcasses of
the dead ram and ewe. Their hides were covered with a mixture
of wool and hair, not wool alone as on domestic sheep. The
quality of the wool, however, was superior to any he had ever
seen. "After parting their beautiful wool on the side and many

places along the back, shoulders, and hips, and examining it closely with my lens, I shouted: 'Well done for wildness! Wild wool is finer than tame!' "[5] He took some wool away with him. The more he pondered it, the more it seemed a parable of civilization's wrong turning. Following a winter's reflection, Muir wrote "Wild Wool," which was published in the spring of 1875.

Anger, stored from childhood, showed in Muir's opening lines. "Moral improvers have calls to preach. I have a friend who has a call to plough, and woe to the daisy sod or azalea thicket that falls under the savage redemption of his keen steel shares." Such a man, Muir accused, reduces living earth to a miserable "chaos of agricultural possibilities calling for grubbing-hoes and manures." Yet this man believes he is improving nature, taking the rough and making something fine from it; he quotes the proverb, "Culture is an orchard apple; Nature is a crab."

Offering wild wool as evidence, Muir affirmed the opposite: "All wildness is finer than tameness." He explained that nature takes better care of her children than does human culture. They are all appropriately clothed, and "she never allows them to go dirty or ragged." The only virtue of the domestic sheep, Muir continued, is that while yielding inferior wool, it gives a far larger quantity. This advantage, however, benefits not the sheep—who has been reduced to a sorry creature—but only humanity. To achieve this single benefit, the sheep is degraded and the environment despoiled. At the root of this deterioration, argued Muir, is an inappropriate standard of evaluation:

> No dogma taught by the present civilization seems to form so insuperable an obstacle in the way of a right understanding of the relations which culture sustains to wildness as that which regards the world as made especially for the uses of man. . . .
>
> I have never yet happened upon a trace of evidence that seemed to show that any one animal was ever made for another as much as it was made for itself.

Muir's analysis anticipated the modern ecological perspective. To say that each creature is made for itself and has

intrinsic value is not to suggest that creatures are isolated from
each other, but quite the opposite. "In the making of every
animal the presence of every other animal has been recognized." They fit together so that the life of all supports the life of
each. This complex of life-support allows individuality to flourish. Remove creatures from a vital ecology and they become
dull stereotypes, like domesticated sheep or industrial humanity. "Were it not for the exercise of individualizing cares on the
part of Nature, the universe would be felted together like a
fleece of tame wool."

The climax of Muir's argument is a striking paradox:
when we are domesticated we are alienated from each other,
but when we are wild we are in touch most deeply with other
life. The engagement of expressive selves, in an ecological context, sustains all.

> . . . we are governed more than we know, and most when we are
> wildest. Plants, animals, and stars are all kept in place, bridled
> along appointed ways, *with* one another and *through the midst*
> of one another—killing and being killed, eating and being
> eaten, in harmonious proportions and quantities. And it is right
> that we should thus reciprocally make use of one another, rob,
> cook, and consume, to the utmost of our healthy abilities and
> desires. Stars attract one another as they are able, and harmony
> results. Wild lambs eat as many wild flowers as they can find or
> desire, and men and wolves eat the lambs to just the same
> extent.

Humanity may reenter this ecology if we can achieve
"healthy abilities and desires." At present, human abilities and
selfish desires overwhelm other life. The path to health, Muir
was convinced, is to establish new relationships with nature,
relationships which are not primarily economic or exploitative,
but sensuous, loving, and respectful. Such integrating relationships must become primary if human economic needs are to be
met within a healthy ecology. Given the rate at which wildness
is being subdued by technology, the only hope for person or
beast is for humans to discover love for nature. This is, indeed,
a call for new birth.

Muir concluded his essay with a proposal to improve domestic sheep by crossbreeding them with wild. This was his suggestion for humanity as well: "A little pure wildness is the one great present want, both of men and sheep."

* * *

Muir's vision was more than a precocious ecological insight. It was a religious vision, a peaceable kingdom, responsive to Isaiah's prophecy.

> Then the wolf shall live with the sheep,
>   and the leopard lie down with the kid;
> the calf and the young lion shall grow up together,
> and a little child shall lead them;
>   the cow and the bear shall be friends,
>   and their young shall lie down together.
> The lion shall eat straw like cattle;
> the infant shall play over the hole of the cobra,
> and the young child dance over the viper's nest.
> They shall not hurt or destroy in all my holy mountain;
>   for as the waters fill the sea,
> so shall the land be filled with the knowledge of the LORD.
>   (Isaiah 11:6-9, NEB)

Muir would agree with Isaiah that when all creatures have a godly perspective, they will not fear relationships with other creatures, relationships which tend to sustain the life of each. Humanity will be companion to nature. None will dominate. The "little child" who leads in Isaiah's vision is not a human tyrant but, Christians believe, the Christ: God as gentle persuader, God vulnerable to creation, God among the creatures. This is the God Muir knew and loved.

Muir's vision differed from Isaiah's in that he accepted the ecology of eating and being eaten. Isaiah imagined that, for earthly peace to be achieved, God must modify this ecology. The two men differed in part because Muir saw life more comprehensively than did Isaiah. He recognized life in the grass as well as in the kid; therefore peaceableness could not be achieved simply by substituting grass for goat in the diet of the lion. Muir had also communed more deeply with nature than

had Isaiah, prophet of the Jerusalem temple. He saw how ecological relationships protect and build life—how the earth as
God made it is already good, just as God said in Genesis. Isaiah
imagined tranquilizing the wolf to lay him next to domestic
sheep; Muir wished to free the sheep to run wild in the mountains again—in spite of the wolf. Muir believed that the free life
with the hazard of an occasional wolf was more beautiful and
more truly peaceful than the prisons of domestication, however
well shepherded.

Those who denigrate nature for its violence are making
an implicit comparison with the civility of human culture. They
believe culture is more peaceful. In the late twentieth century
this comparison is no longer convincing, for human culture has
become far more violent than ecological systems. We may not
be safer in the wilderness than in our own homes, as Muir suggested, but wilderness is certainly safer than our city streets,
and much safer than our wars. These afflictions, to which we
subject our fellow humans, are exceeded by our treatment of
other species and our abuse of the environments which sustain
life. Compared with the practices of human society, nature by
itself is relatively peaceful.

The point is not that individuals should flee human society and take up life in the wild. If that had been Muir's conviction, he would have remained in the mountains. Rather, the
point is that wildness suggests standards relevant to the development of human culture and critical to the interaction of culture with nature. Wildness is ecological: each living thing has a
place, vulnerable to all yet sustained by all. Each contributes to
the life of all. Culture at its best may also be ecological, nurtur-
ing interdependent diversity. In the finest human culture we
respect one another, and all benefit from the contribution of
each. But when patterns of domination grow within human culture, they also find expression in human relations with nature:
both the oppressor and the oppressed afflict the earth.

For human relationships with nature to enrich both culture and the natural ecology, we must maintain respect for the
characteristics of nature as it is given us by God. When we

make changes in species or ecologies, we take on profound new responsibilities—not just for human life, but for the natural lives and systems we affect. "God takes care of everything that is wild," Muir said, "but he only half takes care of tame things."[6] We cannot evaluate such responsibilities without a standard for reference. Muir suggests that wildness provides a standard: the living ecology is a relevant vision.

"Orchard apples are to me the most eloquent words that culture has ever spoken," Muir allowed, "but they reflect no imperfection upon Nature's spicy crab."[7] Genetic manipulation may indeed "improve" a natural species. The improvements make the fruit, grain, or beast more useful to humanity. In most cases, though, this selection also makes the species more dependent upon us. It is more vulnerable to predator or disease; it requires more fertilizer or irrigation or human protection. Most "improved" species do not survive well in the wild, because they are ecologically dependent upon human culture. While we benefit from them, they add to our practical and moral responsibilities.

Many such genetic improvements neither enhance ecological diversity nor contribute to the health of the earth. In fact, the effect is often the reverse. Hybrid grains are planted in vast monocultures, vulnerable to disease, requiring chemical sprays which poison other life. Herds of sheep, replacing a diverse animal population, denude the landscape. Crop yields per acre are raised by using petroleum-based fertilizer, an increasingly expensive luxury which itself damages living soil structure. Fertilized soil becomes dependent on the chemical fix.

Sometimes there is no real gain at all. Muir tolerantly conceded that "we need not go mourning the buffaloes. In the nature of things they had to give place to better cattle, though the change might have been made without barbarous wickedness."[8] He conceded too soon. My friend Steve Charter, a Montana rancher, is convinced that the original giant herds of antelope and buffalo that evolved along with the prairies stimulated grass growth by their grazing patterns. They converted grasslands into meat more efficiently than modern fenced cattle, and thus, the prairie could produce more meat then than now. White settlers, however, preferred cattle because they were familiar, easier to fence and control. They also fit patterns of private property brought from Europe. Rather than learning creative adaptations to a new environment, which might have yielded more human food, we killed off those we did not understand.

Muir's call to breed back wildness anticipated the most promising new directions in contemporary agricultural research. At the Land Institute in Kansas, Wes Jackson now leads a team who are researching the original prairie grasses in the hope of developing polycultures, including perennial feed grains, which may yield wheats for human harvest without annual plowing, irrigation, or artificial fertilizers. "[T]he best agriculture for any region," Jackson affirms, "is the one that best mimics the region's natural ecosystems."[9]

*   *   *

When John Muir married Louie Strentzel, he assumed management of her father's fruit ranch. Strentzel, an immigrant from Poland, was the pioneer orchardist in the Alhambra Valley of California. He developed the first pear orchards and vineyards, organized the farmers into a grange, and widely promoted fruits as a superior complement to grain farming. When he retired in favor of his new son-in-law, he was a prosperous leader in a diverse agricultural economy that included thousands of acres of apples, pears, peaches, apricots, oranges, grapes, cherries, and mulberries. Here was an opportunity for Muir to continue the exploration of new approaches to agriculture.

However, it was an opportunity to which Muir was constitutionally incapable of response. This was simply not his calling. He drove himself compulsively, though he would not tolerate cruelty to other creatures. ("Muir had the best horses in the valley," a ranch hand recalled. "If you . . . mistreated them in any way, you were fired on the spot."[10]) He reduced the once innovative ranch to a simple commercial enterprise.

Abandoning Strentzel's horticultural experiments, Muir plowed up pastures to extend orchards and vineyards, but confined production to fewer species, mainly pears, Tokay grapes, and cherries. The ranch prospered, assuring Muir's comfort into his old age, but Muir himself languished. He wrote,"I am degenerating into a machine for making money. I am learning nothing in this trivial world of men. I must break away and get out into the mountains to learn the news."[11] Fortunately, at Louie's urging, he did so.

Though he himself would not farm creatively, Muir brooded about the style of farming in California. The earliest farms, like the gold rush mines, had been rapacious. Despite his own experience, however, Muir retained a pastoral hope that some homesteaders, settling amid such beauty, might be calmed and opened to nature.

> Travel-worn pioneers, who have been tossed about like boulders in flood-time, are thronging hither as to a kind of terrestrial heaven, resolved to rest. They build, and plant, and settle, and so come under natural influences. When a man plants a tree he plants himself.[12]

Muir wrote of one "joyful set of farmers" who developed their own irrigation system, though he worried that large companies were monopolizing water by developing the best ditches and refusing to sell to independent farmers.[13] His most ambitious proposal for agricultural reform was to replace the herds of sheep in the Sierra foothills with "thousands of bee-ranches" to produce honey by exploiting, but not damaging, the flowery abundance.[14] But Muir could not respond to his own opportunity to pioneer in agriculture. Culture, and personal history, can limit the perception of even the most sensitive. Besides Muir was called to complete his witness for wilderness.

* * *

I share Muir's ecological populism, his belief that "when light comes, the heart of the people is always right."[15] Humanity and nature were made for each other. We are not inherently alien. Not created to be an abusive species, humanity finds true fulfillment in communion: with God, with other persons, and with the many lives and rich fabric of nature. Nevertheless, we have become abusive with patterns of exploitation which have taken root in our culture. They have become second nature. They affect our understanding of ourselves and distort our capacities. Within a culture of exploitation, the heart of the people may grow cold.

Muir developed one antidote to this acculturation, his tourist strategy. People could be induced to visit nature at times when they were not blinded by personal economic anxiety. Standing apart from their need to earn a living, people were more susceptible to the charms of the wild, more able to open themselves to new relationships. Muir even flirted with the idea of "compulsory recreation" to break the chains of social conditioning.

> Pausing in my studies this peaceful afternoon, I chance to think of the thousands needing rest—the weary in soul and limb, toilers in town and plain, dying for want of what these grand old woods can give. . . . The hall and the theater and the church have been invented, and compulsory education. Why not add compulsory recreation? . . . How hard to pull or shake people out of town![16]

Cultural change will indeed require a recreational strategy, and many other strategies as well: economic, social, political, religious. Nature needs social protection and political rights. Nature also needs to be included in our religious understanding— part of our faith, part of our worship. We must replace the *humanocentrism* of our culture with a perspective which includes all life. Our entire culture needs to be born over again into an inclusive, peaceable kingdom.

This task seems formidable, perhaps impossible. But it is a task which yields immediate satisfactions when we open our eyes to the beauty of the earth. Although change is difficult and sometimes painful, this is not the type of revolution which promises struggle today with satisfactions deferred to an indefinite tomorrow. The joys begin as soon as we are baptized and enter the full stream of life.

10. *John Baptist*

Was John Muir a Christian? If this question means whether he was a loyal player on the team, who identified with the church, then the answer is no. Once he left his father's home, Muir no longer played on the team. Although his wife Louie was a devout Methodist, he did not accompany her to church. The churches he knew were alien to his deepest spirituality. They did not, after all, include bears and water ouzels in their membership—a significant defect, I would agree.

To select a deeper standard, then, was Muir reborn through faith in Jesus Christ? I imagine he would answer that though he admired Jesus, his rebirth came in the wild, through the agency of orchid, sequoia, rock, stream, and glacier. Yet I recognize John Muir as a Christian. I believe nature served as his Christ, leading Muir to know the same God that Jesus revealed.

I prefer to put the question with Calvinist directness, the way Muir himself would best receive it. Did God choose John Muir? Did the Lord employ Muir for godly purposes? Did God speak through Muir to his time? Does God speak through him to our time? My answer to each of these is yes. John Muir was a prophet for the Lord.

A prophet speaks with moral urgency to his or her culture. In the biblical tradition prophets stand outside the priesthood, outside the structure which normally links God with people. A prophet is not an official moral interpreter, but a person who speaks from the passion of insight and the strength of conviction. Though professionals often claim the name, prophets are usually amateurs. Amos was careful to affirm that he was not a professional prophet, speaking for hire, nor a member of the prophetic brotherhood. "I am a herdsman and a dresser of sycomore-figs. But the LORD took me as I followed the flock and said to me, 'Go and prophesy to my people Israel!' So now listen to the word of the LORD" (Amos 7:14-16, NEB).

Often a prophet carries a painful message, one difficult for society to accept. That is why the Lord must generally call someone beyond official circles; prophets speak truths which officials would never imagine. Sometimes, of course, if the situation seems hopeless and the official interpreters are in despair, the Lord may call a prophet to speak a comforting, hopeful word—as did "Second Isaiah" during the Hebrew exile. Although prophets may recall the past and warn of the future, the burden of their message concerns the here and now. They call people to change, to grasp new insight, to act with renewed justice and compassion, to be faithful to the Lord.

Since prophets have no credentials, it is difficult to distinguish a true prophet from a false. In societies open to prophecy, false prophets abound. The hearer must decide, and since prophets are humans, the most genuine may sometimes make mistakes. Does the prophet's message contain fresh insight about a problem in society? Does it show where justice lies? Does it trouble the wicked? Does it inspire compassion? Does the prophet's word help make God plain—alive again amid the needs of this age? Does it empower hearers with insight, and call them to relevant action? Is it, in short, a word of moral beauty?

I hear John Muir speaking as such a prophet, telling us that God wants humans to care for nature and not destroy the systems of life. Muir clarifies for me the Lord's invitation—and permission—to listen to nature. The God whom I first met through Scripture and church now exhibits new facets of vitality. After hearing John Muir, I walk in the world more alertly. I take more delight in God's creation. As my respect for nature grows, my thankfulness to God increases. I am eager to nurture life and protect it from human abuse.

* * *

Muir identified with John the Baptist because the Baptist was a voice from the wilderness—a prophet who lived in the wilderness and heard the Spirit there. Muir may have noticed that the words from Isaiah, which Luke cites to validate the Baptist's ministry, might also be read as a description of glacial action preparing for life.

> The voice of one crying in the wilderness,
> Prepare ye the way of the Lord,
> Make [God's] paths straight.
> Every valley shall be filled,
> And every mountain and hill shall be brought low;
> And the crooked shall be made straight,
> And the rough ways *shall be* made smooth;
> And all flesh shall see the salvation of God.
>
> (Luke 3:4-6, KJV, alt.)

John baptized with water. He claimed that stones could be as elect as God's holy people: "I tell you, God is able from these stones to raise up children to Abraham" (Luke 3:8, RSV). Jesus himself came to receive baptism from this wilderness prophet, a fact which may have reassured Muir. In the Baptist he found a model for his own sense of vocation, though Muir would speak not just from the wilderness but also on behalf of the wilderness, calling the people to repentance.

The Baptist prepared the way for the Lord, helping people open themselves so they would be ready to hear Jesus. This was not a conscious part of Muir's vocation. In our society, however, there are many like Muir, alienated from the traditional expressions of Christianity. Muir's approach to nature, widely read for a century, has enriched the spirituality of many who do not relate well to the Christian churches. Muir may have helped some of these meet the God in whom Christians also believe. Muir's words were not addressed to the church as such, but to American society. He is similar in this respect to other Americans who, I believe, have spoken prophetically: Thomas

Jefferson, Abraham Lincoln, Martin Luther King. A prophet usually speaks to the whole society.

However, in these reflections I have suggested particular implications of Muir's insights for Christians. Muir correctly recognized that Christian churches in his day made a larger contribution to environmental degradation than to harmonious relationships with nature. They did this by urging their members to disregard the world, seen as a source of temptation, at the same time as they affirmed human rights of mastery over nature. The resulting message encouraged exploitation: "Don't notice, but do what you wish with nature." The behavior of Muir's father caricatured this norm.

In contrast to this, I have suggested that Christians may responsibly rebuild religious and ethical relationships with the natural world. Natural life belongs in Christian theology—and not just considered under "stewardship," as though our only significant relationship with nature is as managers. All species and living systems are beneficiaries of God's creative delight and our Lord's redemptive intention. Natural life and ecosystems should receive as prominent attention in Christian ethics as do the poor and oppressed peoples. Their situations are comparable. Christ waits with them for us.

While churches are rethinking theology to remove patterns of patriarchy, authoritarianism, racism, and sexism, we should also reform *humanocentrism*. Each of these patterns of oppression has similar roots, and each supports the others. All these patterns, I believe, contradict the deepest teachings of Scripture and the example of Jesus. To overcome any of these sins, we must work to overcome all of them together.

Churches may include nature in worship. I do not suggest that Christians should worship nature, but we may certainly gather consciously in the presence of all life. As the psalm encourages, we, with all creation, may praise the Lord together.

> O praise the LORD. . . .
> Praise [the LORD], sun and moon,

> Praise, all you shining stars; . . .
> Praise the LORD from the earth,
>   you water-spouts and ocean depths;
> fire and hail, snow and ice,
>   gales of wind obeying [God's] voice;
> all mountains and hills,
>   all fruit-trees and all cedars;
> wild beasts and cattle,
>   creeping things and winged birds;
> kings and all earthly rulers, . . .
> young men and maidens,
>   old . . . and young together.
> Let all praise the name of the LORD.
>
> (Psalm 148, NEB, alt.)

It will take imagination for us to achieve this. Christians need visible, tangible signs that bears and water ouzels are indeed members with them in the same fellowship. We need assurance that it is appropriate to love and enjoy these brothers and sisters from other species. As believers, we have a right to rejoice in the whole fabric of life, understanding how through the world's ecology God has blessed all creatures together. Through new liturgies of faith, old attitudes can be reformed and new appreciation encouraged.

I hope this book will encourage some to read Muir, and especially, I hope it will help some engage nature with sensuous delight and spiritual discernment. Some suggestions for further reading follow this chapter.

This book also introduces a series of books under the general title, *Environmental Theology*. In the next book I develop an understanding of the beauty of the Lord to help us awaken our senses and dissolve impediments to expressive relationships with natural life. The third book is a biblical ecology, suggesting how the Old and New Testaments convey God's delight in nature, the place of nature in God's saving purpose, and the human vocation to nurture other forms of life. I present, in the fourth book, a proposal to reform American culture by recognizing constitutional rights for species and environmental systems, and I develop implications for personal ethics, social policy, and agriculture.

*   *   *

In our pluralist society, strong secular organizations are essential to promote experience with nature and coordinate political action to defend nature's interests. The Sierra Club, the organizational expression of John Muir's legacy, has been magnificently effective. I hope every Christian joins such a group as part of an environmental witness.

However, social action and environmental protection do not encompass all of Muir's legacy. The Sierra Club has adopted a motto from Henry David Thoreau: "In wildness is the preservation of the world." Muir preferred to say, "In God's wildness lies the hope of the world."[1] Muir's message, while never sectarian, was fundamentally religious. Preservation is essential, but beyond preservation is the hope of communion and delight, sensuous and spiritual experience. Wilderness is sacramental: it can help us meet God.

Muir had a caution applicable to both ecological and religious enthusiasts: when we feel we know our goal and rush toward it, we may miss the life on the way. Muir could move swiftly across wild country, but his approach was characteristically relaxed, open, exploratory. His favorite word for wilderness activity was "sauntering." " 'Hiking' is a *vile* word," he said. "You should saunter through the Sierra."[2] We are not likely to arrive personally at our goals for social or religious reform. Nevertheless, the style of our travel will have its impact. Muir was sensitive to the fact that each thing we do eventually touches everything else in the world, however lightly. Our goals are in our imaginations, but our means ripple through the world. Therefore the means we use should anticipate the special qualities of the goals we seek. Let our walk be joyful, open, full of communion, receptive as well as expressive. Let us permit ourselves, like Muir, to "stand in what all the world would call an idle manner, literally gaping with all the mouths of soul and body, demanding nothing, fearing nothing, but hoping and enjoying enormously."[3]

* * *

On Christmas Eve, 1914, at age seventy-six, John Muir died from double pneumonia. That is the fact, as we note facts. But the truth is more. Muir said it best in his journal note on the Yosemite bear he found dead by the trail:

> ... he has terrestrial immortality. His life not long, not short, knows no beginning, no ending. To him life unstinted, unplanned, is above the accidents of time, and his years, markless and boundless, equal Eternity.[4]

Muir's "terrestrial immortality" continues. In 1897 Muir had complained that "there is not a single specimen of the redwood in any national park."[5] A decade later William Kent, angered when a water company sought to condemn for a reservoir a magnificent grove of redwoods he owned across the Golden Gate from San Francisco, donated the grove to the federal government to be named Muir Woods. In dozens of national parks, national forests, and reserves across the west where trees thrive, streams run clear, and nature rejoices, John Muir remains part of the ecology—as present as the glaciers and the uplifting rocks. His influence helped them stand.

Most surely John Muir lives in Yosemite National Park, that magnificent reserve where wild splendor meets with eager tourists. It is a realistic meeting. Though Hetch Hetchy is blotted by a fluctuating reservoir, and the Yosemite valley is crowded with people and is sometimes hazy from campfires and automobile exhaust, much of the wildness and most of the beauty remain. Nature lives here abundantly. People meet nature intimately, at many elevations, in many ways. I believe that culture is changed more by Yosemite than Yosemite by culture, though the cultural changes diffuse through society, while those in Yosemite cluster more visibly. As Muir wished, the Yosemite ecology brings people and nature together for the salvation of each.

If Muir had one favorite spot it was the place he called "Sunnyside Bench," a narrow shelf part way up the canyon wall to the east of Yosemite Falls, overlooking the valley.[6] He often retreated there, sometimes for the night. As he sat there at sunset on March 14, 1873, pondering mortality, he wrote:

> We seem to imagine that since Herod beheaded John the Baptist, there is no longer any voice crying in the wilderness. But no one in the wilderness can possibly make such a mistake, for every one of these flowers is such a voice. No wilderness in the world is so desolate as to be without divine ministers. God's love covers all the earth as the sky covers it, and also fills it in every pore. And this love has voices heard by all who have ears to hear.[7]

Suggestions for Reading

John Muir is a delight to read, and better collections of his writings are now in print than during his lifetime, including selections from his notebooks, letters, and journals. These are often more fresh and intimate than his polished articles.

I recommend beginning with *To Yosemite and Beyond: Writings from the Years 1863 to 1875*. This is an engaging selection from letters, journals, and published articles written during Muir's intense immersion in wilderness. Excellent notes by Robert Engberg and Donald Wesling give the reader necessary context. Muir is alive in these pages.

The Wilderness World of John Muir, edited by Edwin Way Teale, includes a full range of Muir's published writings, including his boyhood recollections and exciting account of his first summer in the Sierra. Each selection is introduced well. *Wilderness Essays*, a smaller collection, includes "Twenty Hill Hollow" and "Wild Wool."

John Muir Summering in the Sierra, edited by Robert Engberg, is an attractive collection of Muir's earliest published articles, from the San Francisco *Daily Evening Bulletin*, 1874 and 1875.

Of the two books Muir prepared for publication in his lifetime, *The Mountains of California*, still reads well and is available in an attractive edition introduced by Edward Hoagland. These essays present Muir's ecological insights in a comprehensive manner.

When you have fallen in love with Muir, you will treasure *John of the Mountains: The Unpublished Journals of John Muir*. This large, splendid collection edited by Linnie Marsh Wolfe spans from the Yosemite years through Muir's life, and includes fresh, early versions of material Muir later included in polished essays.

Three excellent books about Muir have been published recently. Frederick Turner has written a full biography, *Rediscovering America: John Muir in His Time and Ours*. From his rich knowledge of the nineteenth century, Turner affectingly portrays Muir's family and relationships, and the landscapes which influenced Muir's life. Muir himself does not come to life in this book, but he does in his own writings, and this book provides context which many readers of Muir will want.

In *John Muir and His Legacy*, Stephen Fox begins with a short biography and then traces a fascinating history of the conservation movement to the present day. Here are the preservationist politics Muir inspired, contrasted skillfully with the rival conservationist stream from Muir's contemporary, Gifford Pinchot.

Michael P. Cohen grapples with Muir's philosophy and spirituality in *The Pathless Way: John Muir and American Wilderness*. Written from an American Buddhist perspective, this is the most stimulating study of Muir I have read. I disagreed with it frequently and benefited from it enormously.

Most unpublished Muir papers have been collected at The Holt-Atherton Pacific Center for Western Studies, University of the Pacific, Stockton, California. Ronald Limbaugh and his staff are helpful to the serious student of Muir. A microfilm edition of their collection, and the catalogue to it, are available through inter-library loan.

To remain in contact with Muir's legacy, there is no better way than joining The Sierra Club, 730 Polk Street, San Francisco, CA 94109. This large, nation-wide organization has chapters nearly everywhere, combining wilderness exploration with advocacy for the environment. It publishes *Sierra* magazine, wilderness guides, and books on topical environmental issues.

Notes

Introduction

1. John Muir, from *Thousand-Mile Walk to the Gulf*, as quoted in Michael P. Cohen, *The Pathless Way: John Muir and American Wilderness*, (Madison: University of Wisconsin Press, 1984), 19.
2. This is the perspective of two fine contemporary studies: Stephen Fox, *John Muir and His Legacy: The American Conservation Movement* (Boston: Little, Brown & Co., 1981), which contains a biography of Muir and an analysis of his political influence, and Cohen, *The Pathless Way*, a study of Muir's philosophy from a Buddhist perspective.
3. John Muir, Letter to Jeanne Carr, wife of Muir's former geology teacher at the University of Wisconsin; quoted in Cohen, *Pathless Way*, 122–123. Muir usually wrote with a blithe disregard for consistency in spelling and punctuation, and I have not corrected him, preferring to retain the exuberant charm of his journals and letters.

Chapter 1.   Awakening

1. Such as hanging from his dormer window sill with one finger. See Muir's account of boyhood in Scotland in *The Wilderness World of John Muir*, ed. Edwin Way Teale (Boston: Houghton Mifflin Co., 1954). 12ff.
2. Quoted in Fox, *Muir and His Legacy*, 31.
3. Muir, *Wilderness World*, 17-19.
4. Muir's letter was printed in the *Boston Recorder*, Dec. 21, 1866. Quoted in Fox, *Muir and His Legacy*, 43.
5. Letter to S. Galloway, May 1866, quoted in Fox, *Muir and His Legacy*, 48.
6. Muir, quoted in Fox, *Muir and His Legacy*, 49.
7. Fox, *Muir and His Legacy*, 50.
8. Muir, *Wilderness World*, 89-90.
9. Quoted in Fox, *Muir and His Legacy*, 51.
10. Quoted in Fox, *Muir and His Legacy*, 52.
11. Quoted in Fox, *Muir and His Legacy*, 52.
12. Muir, *Wilderness World*, 96.

13. John Muir, *To Yosemite and Beyond: Writings from the Years 1863 to 1875*, ed. Robert Engberg and Donald Wesling (Madison: University of Wisconsin Press, 1980), 37.

14. Muir, Journal of June 6, 1869, *Yosemite and Beyond*, 51.

15. Muir, *Yosemite and Beyond*, 19.

16. Muir, *Yosemite and Beyond*, 88.

17. John Muir, *The Yosemite* (Garden City: Doubleday, Anchor Books, 1962), 20.

18. Muir, *Yosemite and Beyond*, 57.

19. Muir, *Yosemite and Beyond*, 137-138.

20. Muir, *Yosemite and Beyond*, 53.

21. John Muir, *John of the Mountains: The Unpublished Journals of John Muir*, ed. Linnie Marsh Wolfe (Madison: University of Wisconsin Press, 1979), 69.

22. Muir, *Yosemite and Beyond*, 52.

23. Muir, *Yosemite and Beyond*, 145-146.

24. Muir, *Yosemite and Beyond*, 159.

25. Jonathan Edwards, Misc. 108, quoted in Roland André Delattre, *Beauty and Sensibility in the Thought of Jonathan Edwards: An Essay in Aesthetics and Theological Ethics* (New Haven: Yale University Press, 1968), 181.

26. Muir, *Yosemite and Beyond*, 113.

27. Muir, *Yosemite and Beyond*, 65-66. This fragment is undated, but the language parallels a letter to Muir's brother dated June 4, 1871.

28. Muir, *Yosemite and Beyond*, 69-70.

29. Muir, *Yosemite and Beyond*, 75.

Chapter 2.   Christ in Nature

1. Muir, *Yosemite and Beyond*, 10-11.

2. Letter to J. B. McChesney, January 9, 1873, John Muir Papers, Holt-Atherton Center for Western Studies, University of the Pacific. Copyright 1984 Muir-Hanna Trust, no. 00195.

3. Muir, *Yosemite and Beyond*, 17.

4. Cohen, *Pathless Way*, 122.

5. Muir, quoted in Cohen, *Pathless Way*, 41.

6. Muir, *Yosemite and Beyond*, 118.

7. Muir, *Yosemite and Beyond*, 61.

Chapter 3.   Spirituality

1. Muir, *John of the Mountains*, 83-84.

2. Muir, *John of the Mountains*, 137-138.

3. Muir, Journal of 1872, John Muir Papers, no. 00006, 128. Here, and elsewhere when necessary in rendering Muir's unpublished notes, I have changed his abbreviations to complete words and sentences.
4. Muir, *John of the Mountains*, 90.
5. Muir, *John of the Mountains*, 79-80.
6. Muir, *Wilderness World*, 166.
7. Muir, *Yosemite and Beyond*, 119.
8. Muir, quoted in Cohen, *Pathless Way*, 134.
9. Muir, *The Yosemite*, 64-65.
10. Muir, quoted in Cohen, *Pathless Way*, 138.
11. Muir, *Yosemite and Beyond*, 125.
12. John Muir, *The Mountains of California* (New York: Viking Penguin Inc., 1985), 175.
13. Muir, *Mountains of California*, 176.
14. Muir, *Mountains of California*, 177.
15. Cohen, *Pathless Way*, 142.

Chapter 4. Sensuousness

1. Muir, *Mountains of California*, 89, 90.
2. Cohen, *Pathless Way*, 40, 219.
3. Muir, *Wilderness World*, 162-165.
4. Muir, *Mountains of California*, 91.
5. Muir, *John of the Mountains*, 88.
6. Muir, *John of the Mountains*, 226.
7. Letter to Catherine Merrill, July 12, 1871, John Muir Papers.
8. Letter to Catherine Merrill, June 9, 1872, John Muir Papers.
9. Wilhelm Reich, *The Function of the Orgasm* (New York: Simon and Schuster, 1972), 272-286.
10. Edward W. L. Smith, *The Body in Psychotherapy* (Jefferson, NC: McFarland & Co., Inc., 1985), 3-33.
11. Letter of October 14, 1872, quoted in Cohen, *Pathless Way*, 39.
12. John Muir, *John Muir Summering in the Sierra*, ed. Robert Engberg (Madison: University of Wisconsin Press, 1984), 109.
13. See Muir, *The Yosemite*, 148-172.
14. S. Hall Young, quoted in Frederick Turner, *Rediscovering America: John Muir in His Time and Ours* (New York: Viking Penguin Inc., 1985), 256-257.
15. Muir, *John of the Mountains*, 170.
16. Muir, *Summering in the Sierra*, 149.
17. Muir, *John of the Mountains*, 53.

Chapter 5.   Moral Beauty

1. I develop this understanding in *Beauty of the Lord: Awakening the Senses*, Book 2 of this theology. A philosophical portion of my definition may be found in Richard Cartwright Austin, "Beauty: A Foundation for Environmental Ethics," *Environmental Ethics* 7 (Fall 1985): 197ff.
2. Muir, quoted in Cohen, *Pathless Way*, 81. See chapter 1, above, for the climax of Muir's climb on Mount Ritter. A full account of this trip is in Muir, *Mountains of California*, 34–51.
3. Muir, Journal of 1872, John Muir Papers, no. 00006, 3-6.
4. John Muir, *Our National Parks* (Madison : University of Wisconsin Press, 1981), 4.

Chapter 6.   Baptism

1. Muir, *John of the Mountains*, 102-103. From Journal of January 6, 1873.
2. Muir, quoted in Cohen, *Pathless Way*, 81, and above in Chapter 5.
3. Muir, "Twenty Hill Hollow," in *Wilderness Essays* (Salt Lake City, UT: Peregrine Smith, Inc., 1980), 70-88. All subsequent quotations in this section are from this essay.
4. Letter to David G. Muir, April 10, 1870, John Muir Papers, no. 00505.
5. Muir, *Summering in the Sierra*, 62.
6. Muir, *Mountains of California*, 159. Here begins Muir's principal essay on the Douglas squirrel, though he also used the Douglas squirrel in many other essays on the Sierra forest.
7. Muir, quoted in Cohen, *Pathless Way*, 122-123.
8. Muir, *Mountains of California*, 161.
9. Muir, *Mountains of California*, 168. Muir goes on to note that he tried the same musical program again another year, with the same result.
10. Muir, *Mountains of California*, 191, 192. This is Muir's principal essay on the ouzel.
11. Muir, *John of the Mountains*, 130.
12. Muir, *Mountains of California*, 199-200, 201, 207.
13. Muir, *John of the Mountains*, 177-178.
14. Muir, *Mountains of California*, 219-220.
15. Muir, *Summering in the Sierra*, 40-46.
16. Muir, *Wilderness Essays*, 70, and above.
17. Muir, *Mountains of California*, 225.
18. Muir, quoted in Cohen, *Pathless Way*, 174.

Chapter 7. Glacial Eye

1. Muir, *Mountains of California*, 48.
2. Muir, *John of the Mountains*, 213.
3. Muir, *John of the Mountains*, 168.
4. Muir, *John of the Mountains*, 213.
5. Muir, *John of the Mountains*, 82-83.
6. Muir, *Yosemite and Beyond*, 162.
7. Muir, quoted in Cohen, *Pathless Way*, 60.
8. Muir, holograph ms. ("Philosophy and Religion"), ca. 1870, John Muir Papers, no. 08514.
9. Muir, *John of the Mountains*, 72.
10. I will develop the biblical basis for this perspective in Book 3 of this series.

Chapter 8. Prophecy

1. Muir, quoted in Turner, *Rediscovering America*, 225.
2. Muir, *Yosemite and Beyond*, 155.
3. Muir, *Yosemite and Beyond*, 159.
4. See Turner, *Rediscovering America*, 201-209.
5. Muir, *John of the Mountains*, 94-95.
6. Muir, quoted in Fox, *Muir and His Legacy*, 73.
7. Muir, quoted in Fox, *Muir and His Legacy*, 104-105.
8. Samuel Merrill, quoted in Fox, *Muir and His Legacy*, 107.
9. Muir, quoted in Fox, *Muir and His Legacy*, 120.
10. Muir, quoted in Turner, *Rediscovering America*, 318.
11. Muir, quoted in Cohen, *Pathless Way*, 221-222.
12. Muir, *Our National Parks*, 1, 19, 28.
13. Pinchot, quoted in Turner, *Rediscovering America*, 303.
14. Muir, *Our National Parks*, 330, 332, 337, 360.
15. Muir, *Our National Parks*, 352, 357.
16. Muir, *Our National Parks*, 348.
17. Muir, *Our National Parks*, 363.
18. Muir, *Our National Parks*, 33-34.
19. Fox, *Muir and His Legacy*, 125.
20. Fox, *Muir and His Legacy*, 128-129.
21. This and subsequent quotes from Muir concerning Hetch Hetchy are from the chapter on "Hetch Hetchy Valley" in *The Yosemite*, 192-202. Muir rushed this book to print in 1912 during the height of the Hetch Hetchy controversy.
22. Muir, quoted in Turner, *Rediscovering America*, 342-343.

Chapter 9.   Agriculture

1. This homesteading childhood is affectingly recreated in Turner, *Rediscovering America*, 28-79.
2. Muir, *John of the Mountains*, 351.
3. Muir, in Cohen, *Pathless Way*, 200.
4. Muir, *Mountains of California*, 210, 211.
5. This and subsequent quotes in this section are from Muir's essay "Wild Wool," in *Wilderness Essays*, 227-242.
6. Muir, *Yosemite and Beyond*, 121.
7. Muir, *Wilderness Essays*, 239.
8. Muir, *Our National Parks*, 335.
9. Wes Jackson and Marty Bender, "Investigations into Perennial Polyculture," 183-194 in Wes Jackson, Wendell Berry, and Bruce Colman, eds., *Meeting the Expectations of the Land: Essays in Sustainable Agriculture and Stewardship* (San Francisco: North Point Press, 1984), 183. I will discuss agricultural issues more comprehensively in Book 4 of this theology.
10. R. J. Ryan, *John Muir Historic Site*, (Point Reyes, California, 1977), quoted in Turner, *Rediscovering America*, 270, note.
11. Muir, quoted in Turner, *Rediscovering America*, 272. My description of Muir's fruit ranching is drawn from this biography.
12. Muir, in Cohen, *Pathless Way*, 226.
13. Muir, *Summering in the Sierra*, 139-142.
14. "The Bee-Pastures," *Mountains of California*, 234ff.
15. Muir, in Turner, *Rediscovering America*, 318.
16. Muir, *John of the Mountains*, 234.

Chapter 10.   John Baptist

1. Muir, quoted in Paul Brooks, *Speaking for Nature* (San Francisco: Sierra Club Books, 1983), 19.
2. Muir, quoted in Fox, *Muir and His Legacy*, 120.
3. Muir, *John of the Mountains*, 102-103.
4. Muir, *John of the Mountains*, 83.
5. Muir, *Our National Parks*, 351.
6. Location according to an editorial note in Muir, *Yosemite and Beyond*, 128.
7. Muir, *John of the Mountains*, 135-136.

Index

BIBLICAL CITATIONS